BOLD BODY LANGUAGE

Win Everyday with Nonverbal Communication Secrets. A Beginner's Guide on How to Read, Analyze, and Influence Other People. Master Social Cues, Detect Lies, and Impress with Confidence

Gerard Shaw

FREE GIFT

This book includes a bonus booklet. Download may be for a limited time only. All information on how you can secure your gift right now can be found at the end of this book.

TABLE OF CONTENTS

INTRODUCTION

Would you like to influence others and forge deeper connections with them? Maybe you have a friend who always seems to accurately read the room or know what someone is thinking. Interested in public speaking or presenting, but worried that your nervousness would be too obvious?

Do you have great ideas but can't seem to get them across? Maybe it's because your body language is giving them the wrong message. Or perhaps theirs is telling you something that you can't quite figure it out. Did you notice what they were trying to "say" to you without actually speaking?

If you find yourself struggling with any of the issues above, then this book will help you solve these problems. You'll learn what body language is and how it's used. More importantly, you'll find information that you can actually use in your own life: how to read what another person is conveying to you with their body and how to use your own body to convey information. Get the results you want, just by practicing nonverbal communication.

Have you ever looked in the mirror and thought, *Boy, I have got it going on today!* Maybe you were dressed up for an event. I remember going to a party just out of college. I had just bought a motorcycle at the time, and I arrived in my biking gear. I looked cool. And I remember people turning to look at me all night—noticing me, paying attention to me. It wasn't that I'd suddenly transformed into a James Dean-esque character with my leather jacket. But I felt confident, and that's what everyone was responding to. I

1

walked into the room with my head held high.

The best part is, you don't have to put on new clothes. You don't ever necessarily have to feel confident. You just have to project confidence fo people to notice and pay attention to you. Maybe you're not a big partygoer but you want your boss to notice you more at work. Or maybe you're giving a presentation, and you want people to pay attention.

Want to know these secrets? I wrote this book because I have learned how to work my own body language with great results. I've combined my own experience with science and proven data, and I share all this with you in the book as well. I've increased my ability to develop deep relationships with others. These connections have provided me with an amazing network of people in both my personal and business life. My effective communication has also brought in a steady flow of opportunities.

The knowledge of body language and how to use it is backed up by scientific studies. I don't go into the theoretical aspects in depth because that doesn't bring the success people want. (I leave all the theorizing to the PhDs.) Instead, I have a book full of practical advice. Once you absorb the knowledge, you can apply it using the techniques I provide in this book.

I'm passionate about the advantages of nonverbal communication and strongly believe that knowing how to skillfully utilize and interpre nonverbal cues can change your life for the better. And it's not just me! I've heard the testimonies of others and seen the transformation that takes place when people learn to "speak" nonverbally. People who used the knowledge in this book acquired a whole new vocabulary they didn't have before. They project confidence and success not just professionally, but in all aspects o

2

fe. Everyone benefits when our messages are delivered correctly and with ewer misunderstandings.

By reading this book and putting the actionable steps in place, you too an become more successful day by day. I have collected a wealth of aluable information that will help you improve your communication skills s well as your style and people skills. Presenting yourself to others, even nose whom you don't know, doesn't have to be a difficult ordeal!

This book is for anyone who wants to be successful in any aspect of neir lives, whether it's their relationships, professional career, or just to chieve the goal or purpose they've set for themselves. Many young adults ely on email and social media to stay in touch. But real life requires you to how up in person too. Survival in today's world isn't just about the words ou use. It's how you convey your message when you're talking to other eople.

Words are only part of what you're saying. The rest of your body ontributes too. In fact, most face-to-face communication takes place hrough your visual senses, not your auditory ones. The techniques in this ook show you how to move (or not move!) depending on what you want o say. When you choose to sit closer to someone, you'll know exactly what ou're telling them. When you cross your arms, the message you're sending vill be deliberate.

You'll learn how to read other people since reading body language is a kill that can be learned just like reading a book or riding a bicycle. And, ust like riding a bicycle, the more you practice, the better you'll be. If omeone you're talking to crosses their arms, you'll know what they are actually trying to tell you!

Once you start taking action, you'll see an improvement in your ability to communicate not just with others but with yourself as well. Some nonverbal cues actually produce positive feedback loops for you when you use them. You'll discover how to fake it 'til you make it. For example, the more you use your body to convey confidence, the more self-assured you feel. Others notice this behavior and respond positively to you, which makes you more confident! When you use body language even just to improve your outlook, you'll be amazed at the results.

How do you become more charismatic or stand out in a room? Develop meaningful connections? Speak in public so your audience wants more from you? First, I discuss the science behind body language—how information travels from what you see, hear, smell, taste, and touch to your brain and how this triggers the release of chemicals, both neurotransmitters and hormones, which have varying effects on your body.

Once you learn how the body links to the brain and vice versa, I explain the body language "giveaways" to certain moods and emotions. You'll uncover the secrets to controlling your own reactions. Then, you'll be able to read the reactions of other people. Which parts of the body are the most communicative, and where should you start "reading"? What should you look for in others so you can clarify their message?

At that point, you'll have a pretty solid background on body language in general. Then the book goes into the specifics of how to create engaging presentations, spot deceit in others, become charismatic, and build meaningful relationships.

4

Finally, there are tips and tricks for everyday usage. Body language is a use-it-or-lose-it" type of skill. Your ability to communicate without words nproves the more you work on it, but once you stop, you'll gradually start ɔsing this ability. This isn't a skill to be briefly dabbled with and then ɔrgotten. Fortunately, these steps don't require a lot of intellectual thought, eep meditation, or any other time-consuming process. Communicating onverbally is a habit you'll use for the rest of your life, and it isn't a lesson ıat works better when you delay it.

If you could apply everything you'll learn about nonverbal ommunication right now, you would be opening up opportunities this very ıstant. You would be connecting with other people, even an entire audience ı an honest and deep way…right now.

Interested in changing your life for the better? Then you need to take ction. If you do what you've always done, you'll get what you've always ;otten. As Einstein said, "The definition of insanity is doing the same thing ·ver and over again but expecting a different result."

You don't have to completely change your life or schedule, or overhaul verything you do from morning until night. However, you'll likely need to ıake some adjustments to the movements you make and practice observing ·thers for the messages they're sending without words. But to find those ·pportunities and to have that growth, action must be taken.

Words are important. The right words are key. But let your body get in ·n the action, too, by expressing your message nonverbally.

So keep reading. Find out which steps to take…and then take them.

5

This book comes with a FREE booklet on masterminding a winning routine to improve calmness and your level of confidence daily. Head to the bottom of this book for instructions on how you can secure your copy today.

CHAPTER ONE

The Science of Body Language

You've probably heard of it, but you might be wondering exactly what body language is. Body language is a conversation without speech using facial expressions and physical gestures. The components of body language also include tone of voice, posture, volume, rate of speech, eye contact, and other characteristics. Nonverbal communication is often more important than the words you actually say in terms of getting your message across.

You might not have been paying a lot of attention to body language before, which is okay. But you probably have noticed some extreme examples.

Imagine that you're looking at a person whose head is hanging down. They're slouched, shoulders slumped, and not looking you in the eye. Would you believe them if they said in a monotone, "I'm so happy right now"? Of course not. The way in which they're expressing themselves physically is not that of a happy person.

By contrast, imagine someone standing tall and straight, looking you in the eye, and shaking your hand firmly with a smile on their face. Would you believe them if they said, "I'm so happy right now"? Probably so, because their body language is positive.

Both body language and speech are necessary to communicate. W
learn how to speak in school, from our parents, or perhaps from movies an
TV as well. But we don't often learn how to use our bodies to help us sa
what we mean.

Using body language isn't about changing your personality or becomin
a different person! It's about enhancing your ability to communicate an
expanding your social skills. Body language is not an exact science becaus
it's based on human behavior, and not all individuals will react the sam
way in every situation.

It's both nature and nurture. We've evolved with some aspects of bod
language that may be almost reflexive in nature. These are the behavior
that you might not even be aware you're demonstrating. Other behavior
are taught by culture, so they may differ from country to country.

Nonverbal communication came before speech, so some of it wil
always be with us. Consider animals and how they express some things t
each other without speaking. Charles Darwin began the scientific study o
how humans and other animals communicate nonverbally, and much of th
later science rests on these foundations.

Neuroscience behind body language

The brain controls body movements, both voluntary and involuntary
Humans have a central nervous system that consists of nerves in the spina
cord along with the brain itself. We also have peripheral nerves locate
everywhere else in the body that take inputs and pass them on. For example
when your nose smells a flower, the peripheral nerves involved send signal

8

the spinal cord. These signals will be electrical and/or chemical in nature. The spinal cord then passes the signals to the brain's sensory processing centers and to other functional areas when needed.

Part of the central nervous system is the autonomous nervous system, which is not under conscious control. This system regulates things like breathing, the heart's pumping, and releasing the muscles' energy reserves. It has two parts that work in opposition to each other and keep each other in check.

The sympathetic system increases stimulation and activation. It releases chemicals to accelerate breathing and widen the blood vessels, minimizing blood flow to parts of the body that don't need it in a state of increased alertness, such as the digestive system. Its opposite, the parasympathetic system, comes into play during rest and relaxation: breathing slows, the digestive system is stimulated, etc.

The human brain also contains the prefrontal cortex, which controls decision making, reasoning, and other complex behaviors. When action must be taken, the brain relays this intent back to the motor neurons of the peripheral system. These nerves then signal the appropriate muscles to perform the action.

Obviously, this process takes less time to do than it does to describe! Some actions don't even have to travel up to the brain first. When a reflex nerve is stimulated (hot stove!), the requisite motor neurons are activated (yank your hand back).

The prefrontal cortex is restricted to humans. Other animals don't have

9

one. We do, however, have some parts of the brain in common with other animals. You might have seen these parts referred to as the "lizard" or "reptilian" brain. The older part of the brain is responsible for the "fight-or flight" reflex, and when this part is active, the prefrontal cortex is inactive

That's because we evolved in the African savannah alongside wild animals that could kill us. The people who survived are the ones who ran when they saw lions because their fight-or-flight reflexes activated, not the ones whose prefrontal cortex slowed them down to ask which action to take But how does that fight-or-flight reflex happen?

This reflex is all chemicals and electricity in the brain, believe it or not When nerves connect to each other through electrical signals, they release chemicals known as neurotransmitters. These neurotransmitters can either excite the next nerve ("go") or inhibit it ("no-go"). This system determines which messages continue through the system.

Neurotransmitters come in several forms. In addition to the "go/no-go" switches, they can also affect mood and behavior. Readying the body for action comes in two flavors: norepinephrine (called noradrenaline in the U.K.) and adrenaline (epinephrine). Norepinephrine increases alertness and is at its lowest level in the body during sleep. It focuses attention and speeds up your heart. It's also responsible for anxiety and nervousness. Adrenaline also increases heart rate and speeds up blood flow to your muscles. Anxiety sweatiness, and shakiness are associated with it as well.

Pleasure transmitters include dopamine and serotonin. Neurons release dopamine when you experience pleasure and excitement. Dopamine tells your body to go do more of whatever caused the pleasure. As seen with

10

ddictions, this isn't always a good thing! Serotonin is used in the body for mood and sleep and to fight depression.

Hormones are similar to neurotransmitters. But instead of relaying information between nerves, they work in the bloodstream. Some chemicals, such as adrenaline, can be both hormones and neurotransmitters. t and the hormone cortisol are released when the brain wants to be in a state of awareness. Other hormones include oxytocin, which promotes bonding in humans; androgens, including testosterone, which drive male maturation; and estrogens such as estradiol, which control female maturation.

The neurotransmitters are important in regulating emotions and feelings. Serotonin, for example, can mitigate anger and violence. You'll need to be able to restrain yourself from acting on your emotions if you want to make sure you're sending the right signals for your nonverbal communication. Also, ensure that your emotions aren't getting in the way of the message someone else is trying to send you!

All these systems and chemicals affect your body language. Your brain senses a threat and sends out signals to put your body on alert. However, the part of your brain responsible for the fight-or-flight reflex can't tell the difference between the threat of a tiger and the threat of speaking in public. In both situations, you'll have the same chemical release of adrenaline and cortisol, which speed up your heart and make you nervous, among other things. Later in the book, I'll discuss what you can do to reduce the threat level so you'll be able to be charismatic and confident instead of shaky.

11

Learning about body language

There are some things about humans that cannot be changed. When you're anxious, certain chemical reactions occur. However, humans (and other animals) can be conditioned or trained to associate a stimulus with a reaction.

For example, you've probably heard of Pavlov's dog. In his experiments, Pavlov conditioned dogs to associate food with the ringing of a bell. Over time, whenever the dogs heard a bell, they would start salivating.

There is a biological basis for this behavior. Dogs salivate when it's time for food. Classical conditioning requires a biological basis, whether you're working with dogs or people. Throughout life, people are conditioned, often without knowing it. We're biologically trained to be alert when there are potential threats. For example, the color red is used to signal danger in various ways. When we see red, we often become alert, even unknowingly.

However, people can also learn without a biological basis. This process is known as operant conditioning or learning from experience. It doesn't even have to be your own experience, though that certainly tends to be the best teacher! You can learn from something someone else did or something you read. Human brains use shortcuts to make the work easier. These different types of learning and conditioning affect body language.

They can also help to change habits. Want to have better body language? You'll need to learn them. The best way to do that is for your brain to see that the new behaviors come with positive reinforcements. But first, you eed to understand where the habit comes from. Then, you can take control

f it. Reprogramming your body language has to be done consistently for it

) stick.

'he body parts of body language

There are four main communicators in our bodies that can let other

eople know what we're feeling, no matter what we're actually saying. In

rder to make sure your message is getting across, you need to control these

spects of the body and ensure that they are "saying" what you want them

). Being aware of your body is the first step to improving your nonverbal

ommunication. What is it saying now, and what do you want it to say?

1. Your head—it's not just about your face!

Even your scalp will provide clues to your state of mind. Didn't have
time to brush your hair? You'll look frazzled. Those who are bald
need to be careful of their eyebrows, which are more prominent
when there's no distracting hairline. Brows can be used to express
yourself, but you want to do that consciously.

Tiny movements around the eyes and mouth, known as
microexpressions, can give you away. Whether you're afraid or
deceitful, these little areas can let others know. You'll need to learn
how to control them, and fortunately, you can.

Neither staring at someone nor avoiding eye contact is polite or
sends the message that you're interested in them in a friendly way.
Making the right amount of eye contact is important.

Your chin and neck provide clues too. Jutting your chin out makes

13

you look stubborn. Most people want to improve their bod language so they can be more likable, leading to new opportunitie and friends. Appearing stubborn won't get you there!

A poised person stands with their neck straight, neither slumpin towards the floor nor lifting their face to the ceiling. Either one o those postures sends a message of disinterest or lack of confidence

2. Torso—including hands and arms

Some body language messages mean different things in differer contexts. You'll need to be aware of them when you're "speaking, but also when you're reading others. If you want some sympathy sag a little around your shoulders. But if you're always slumped, thi will be read as unconfidence. Standing straight with your shoulder back is the posture of a happy, confident person.

Arms can be very expressive! Fidgeting makes you look nervous o bored. Arms crossed tightly across your torso? Angry and defensive Hands on hips make you seem arrogant. But they can also make yo feel more confident, so you can stand in this pose in private whe you need a little ego boost.

When you're sitting, the easiest way to adopt a neutral expressio with your hands is to fold them gently in your lap. Palms up is supplicating position.

3. Legs—you know how to use them

While you're sitting, if your legs are tightly crossed, you look close off. An open stance can be welcoming, but don't open so wide as t be sloppy! And if you're male, avoid "manspreading" and taking up too much space in public.

Women wearing skirts have to be careful about how they're sitting. If you're nervous about whether your skirt is too short, pretty soon everyone around you will be as well. Solution: Don't wear skirts that are too short when you're trying to make a good impression. Wearing a longer skirt is easier than constantly worrying if something is exposed. Clothes shouldn't make you fidget.

Are you nervous or anxious in general? This is often expressed by shaking your legs (whether you mean to or not!). Crossing your legs at the ankles is neutral, just like the hands in lap suggestion (assuming appropriate clothing length).

4. Feet

Need to be somewhere? You're probably tapping your feet, but that can come across as rude. A steady stride makes you look confident. Even if you're not feeling very self-assured, you can still move like you are. Plant and pick up your feet as you go.

If you're stumbling, shuffling, or otherwise not moving with good posture, you may seem scared or even shady.

Chapter Summary

- Body language adds or detracts from your speech, depending on how you use it.

- Movements are controlled by the brain through nerves, neurons, neurotransmitters, and hormones.

- While some of our movements are unconscious, others are conscious and we can learn to control them.

- New habits, like that of body language, can be learned through experience.

- There are four areas of the body that are key for nonverbal communication: head, torso, legs, and feet.

In the next chapter, you will learn about the basic process of communication, the barriers to it, and the ways that body language contributes to it.

CHAPTER TWO

Conveying and Receiving the Message

'he communication process isn't quite as simple as one person talking to nother. About three-fourths of any employee's time is spent in iterpersonal situations while at the workplace, and there's often iiscommunication on one side or misinterpretation on the other. Imagine ow much of the message gets lost in each conversation! And if 75% of /ork-life is being conducted this way, how much time and productivity is ist?

One person has to decide the message they want to convey. Then, they hoose the words, the tone, and the way they express it. This may be done learly, or it may not.

Some of these choices aren't always entirely conscious, either. Have ou ever opened your mouth to convey one thing but said something else istead?

Messages are also usually laden with the speaker's emotions, mood, and eelings about the conversation and the people in it, or even those tangential ɔ it. The speaker may still be angry about something that happened earlier nd have it affect an entirely different conversation.

The receiver, meanwhile, must decode the message—not just the word but the context, tone of voice, gestures, and expressions. As a result, th interpretation is sometimes quite different from what the speaker intended The listener may infer contradictory emotions and feelings or might viev the words from a different perspective. They're also influenced by their ow mood and emotions, which may or may not be related to the conversatio at hand.

Sending and receiving isn't only between individuals, either. W communicate with a group of people or an audience as well. Those in th audience or group may also come back with different interpretations of wha the speaker said.

There's a mayor of an American city who often says very quickly, "Gc it," in response to constituents explaining their issues. The phrase can mea different things, so her intent is sometimes unclear. And depending on he normal rate of speech, this could read as dismissive or simply how she talks (She is a fast talker, as it turns out.)

Does she mean, "Got it, I'm not an idiot, you peasant, now sto talking"? Or "Got it, I understand what you're saying, I'll take it back to m office and work on it"? Or "Got it, no more explanation needed, sto talking"? Or "Got it, this is an issue that has been raised several times, bu we haven't been able to find a solution yet"?

If you're feeling annoyed and unheard, you might think she's saying th first one. If you respect her and know that she's working hard for the peopl of your city, you'll likely interpret her message as the last one. Once yo know the basics of body language (which is coming up in Chapter Three) ou'll be able to connect her nonverbal communication to what she's aying.

In other words, it's pretty easy for things to go wrong. The message night not be received in the way it was intended, or even not at all. For xample, the mayor may have said, "Got it," because she now has an wareness of the issue and will have her staff work on it. But you might ave interpreted her as saying, "Shut up, peasant!"

Nonverbal cues can help the receiver decode the message or lead them ɔ a completely different conclusion. That's why it's important to be aware f what you're saying, both verbally and nonverbally, to give your intended nessage. Also, be aware of the meaning behind the signals you receive, so ou can more accurately understand what they want to tell you.

Barriers to communication

When people are talking to each other, there are several obstacles a uccessful message has to overcome, especially when the individuals don't now each other very well. Many of these difficulties can occur within a ulture. Meaning, someone with a South London background can ompletely misunderstand another person from South London, even though hey share the same culture. Therefore, you can't assume that the person istening to you will understand what you're saying just because you have imilar upbringings.

1. Language

No two people experience words in the same way. For example, if someone talks about "the color red," people listening to that person will have unique images in mind for "red." For some people, it ma be a warm-toned red. For others, a blue-red. The color might b lighter or darker from person to person.

With speech, there is plenty of room for interpretation, and n guarantee that the receiver will interpret the words how the sende intended them. A speaker might try to be as descriptive as possible for example, "fire-engine red." Then, everyone whose firefighter drive red trucks will probably have a color close to the speaker' intended one. But those who come from places where the engine are yellow, white, or another color, won't get it.

2. "Perceptual" bias

We're busy! We constantly have a lot of information coming at u that we need to filter through and assess. So, our brains use shortcut or rules of thumb for a lot of the information, just to reduce th amount of work they have to do.

This is where we find stereotypes, self-fulfilling prophecies, an projections. For example, you might stereotype women as bein; uninterested in the sciences. When you're talking to a woman abou a scientific topic, you would assume they know nothing about i You might end up explaining something they already know especially if the woman in question works in the field.

3. Relationships

A past experience with someone will influence how you interpre them. If they came off as arrogant the first time you met, you'l

20

interpret them as being arrogant the next time, even if they're not overbearing at the moment. If you consider them to be dishonest or untrustworthy, you probably won't receive their message as they intended. We're more willing to give the benefit of the doubt to someone who we feel has treated us well in the past.

At work, differences in hierarchy create barriers as well. An employee may interpret their boss saying, "Got it," very differently to a colleague saying the same thing. The person speaking assumes their listeners have the same assumptions they do, which is unlikely to be the case in a large, diverse workforce.

4. Cultural differences

When speaking to someone from a different cultural background, it's very easy to get the message mixed up, especially if the other culture is an unfamiliar one. There are numerous gestures that are polite in one culture and not in another. Or vice versa.

These differences encompass perceptions around privacy, time, and personal space. Some cultures tend to see punctuality as a virtue and see tardiness as a sign of disrespect. Other cultures may place more value on relationships, accepting tardiness to one function because people were enjoying time at another.

Some cultures, particularly those of European heritage, require a larger distance between two people who are interacting (personal space). In other cultures, they may stand much closer, not to infringe upon privacy, but because they're used to being closer when they speak to one another.

Nonverbal communication

Up to 90% of communication between people is nonverbal. Unfortunately, many times, verbal and nonverbal messages are different. The listener has to figure out which is more likely to be the true one in addition to interpreting the actual words being used. Most people will assume that the body language is the true language and reflects what the speaker is feeling, rather than the verbal language.

It's hard for anyone to trust or give the benefit of the doubt to someone who sends mixed messages. The difference between what they say with words and what they say with their body suggests that they have something to hide. It also muddles the message itself. Even if the speaker has nothing to hide, the audience still doesn't know what they mean. Delivering a clear message, the one you want to send, depends on the body language backing up the speech.

Nonverbal communication has four components: visual, tactile, vocal and spatial.

Visual cues include facial expressions, posture, and gestures. These are very important to humans for communication. We evolved to be drawn to other people's faces. Emotions are less likely to be expressed verbally, and more likely to be demonstrated with facial expressions or other body language signals. Humans have had emotions longer than we have had language!

Posture indicates mood and emotion. Unlike some of the other onverbal signals, high-level posture cues are pretty similar across cultures nd ethnicities. A strong stance, with shoulders back and head high, emonstrates self-assurance. Slouching, looking down, covering your rotch with your hands ("fig-leaf" position): this is not a happy or confident erson. The actual mood might range from defensive to nervous to deceitful.

Gestures (at a high level) are key for communication. You might use our hands to emphasize a point you're making or turn your palms up to how that you're not sure of something. Specific gestures can be very easy) misinterpret because so many of them have different meanings across ultures.

Touching the other person is the tactile aspect: a hand on the arm, a hug. hese are often used to indicate interest or caring for the person. It's omething that charismatic people often do. (More detail about charismatic ody language in Chapter Five.) A handshake is also tactile, and a firm one hows self-assurance as well as warmth toward the other person. Crushing andshakes or limp ones send negative signals.

The vocal aspect of body language isn't in the words or language used, ut rather in the intonation and speed of your speech. Imagine saying "Got t" to your teammate when you're playing flag football. Then, "Got it" to our coworker who is droning on and on … and on … about the spreadsheet ou're looking at. Or, "Got it" to your superior, who has just explained to ou why you need to change a cell in that spreadsheet.

Do you think you'd say "Got it" with the same tone of voice to each of he three situations above? Of course not. If you used the same tone with our boss as you did your annoying coworker, you might get fired! You

23

probably would have changed how fast you said the words as well. Quickl dismissive to your coworker, and more slowly to your boss, to show tha you have taken in what they're saying.

The vocal aspect may still be misinterpreted since these also vary acros cultures. What's supportive in one might be quite rude in another. Som languages are spoken much more quickly than others.

The spatial component of body language includes time, space, an image. Arriving early or late for a meeting often sends a specific message Arriving late can signal dominance, dislike, or disinterest. On the othe hand, someone who's interested, either in the topic being discussed or i moving up the career ladder, will usually arrive early to a meeting.

Crowding someone's personal space is also a nonverbal cue. It make people feel uncomfortable, at the very least, possibly even threatened However, this differs very much from culture to culture. Americans, fo example, have a much bigger conception of personal space than man others do. People in the U.S. need about two feet of space from their closes friends and two to four feet for friends. They require even more distanc from strangers. Possibly due to this large amount of personal space Americans also do less interpersonal touching than others.

People also communicate with items, clothing, or other aspects o appearance. Often, "things" signal our values. Someone carrying a high-en designer handbag appears to value luxury. But these cues can also b misinterpreted, so remember to take context into account. If the person i driving a standard, non-luxury car and wearing clothes that aren't designer they may have received the bag as a gift or bought it on sale because they

24

ought it looked pretty.

ive roles of nonverbal language

You now know that much of someone's message is communicated by arious expressions that aren't put into words. Body language can play ifferent roles with verbal communication, either agreeing with it or etracting from it.

1. Repetition

Body language may repeat the message from the words. Your friend says to you, "I'm so happy!" They're smiling, or maybe hugging you. They're standing straight and looking you in the eye.

2. Contradiction

The nonverbal cues may mean the opposite of what's being said. This is where listeners get mixed messages. They have to figure out whether the words or the body is telling the truth. Your friend says to you, "I'm so happy!" But they're not smiling. They're slouching, with eyes on the ground and arms crossed over their chest.

Your friend's words do not match up at all with their body in this case. Which would you believe, their words or their body? That they're happy or unhappy? Most people would choose unhappy, or in other words, the body's speech. And they would probably be right about that!

3. Substitution

Maybe the words don't need to be said at all. Picture someone

rolling their eyes. Do you need words to go with that? This particula
signal seems to be pretty similar across cultures, too.

Or you just got engaged, and you run up to your friend. You thrus
your hand with the ring at them, smiling. There's no real reason t
say the words, "I'm engaged!" unless you just really like how the
sound.

4. Complement

Body language can complement the verbal language. You prais
someone verbally in a meeting, then pat them on the back. It's not
repetition exactly, because a pat on the back isn't necessaril
praising. But obviously, it's a positive movement. You'r
complementing the words with a gesture.

5. Accent

Nonverbal language can underline the point a speaker tries to make
Someone who's passionate about what they're saying might poun
the table, for example. Or if you're angry at what the speaker i
saying, you might throw a shoe while shouting at them.

When you're trying to demonstrate the huge increase in profits the
your product made over the past few months, you could swoop you
hand up.

As an exercise, watch the speaker at your next get-together, whether it'
a meeting or lunch with friends. See if you can tell what the speaker'
gestures mean. Are they accenting the words? Detracting from them? Thi
will help you increase your awareness of body language and its use i

ommunication.

Vhy are nonverbal cues so important?

If you want to influence other people, or develop better relationships nd be more successful, people need to trust you. People do business with 1ose whom they like and trust. And as I noted above, when the verbal 1essage doesn't match the nonverbal cues, you come across as hiding omething. No one trusts a person who seems to be concealing a part of 1emselves.

Most people, when faced with a conflict between the two messages, will ssume that the nonverbal cue is the real one. Are you consciously sending 1ixed signals? Saying one thing but meaning another? If you're not paying ttention to what your body is saying, you have no idea whether you're aying (with your body) what you think you're saying or intend to say. In ddition, you might not be aware of how other people are reacting to you. Aligning what you say in words with the message of your body increases our effectiveness.

Have you ever started ordering something at the coffee shop and got ompletely tongue-tied? Did the order taker still know what you meant? Thanks, body language!

It's also important for you to understand what others are trying to ommunicate with you. If you tend to be a talker, people will start sending ou signals when they want you to finish up: looking away, tapping their oot, yawning, etc. Being aware of these expressions and what they mean an help you be a better conversationalist! And, people will find you less boring when you recognize you're losing your audience and can adjust.

Even if the language is a bit muddled, you can read someone's bod language to figure out what they're trying to say. If they're underlining wha they say by throwing shoes or pounding the table, you'll know they'r passionate about whatever it is they're discussing!

By contrast, you may also be warned when someone is potentiall untrustworthy. They're saying one thing with their words and somethin; totally different with their bodies. They may just be unaware of what they'r saying, but you'll still have to try to sort out which is the true message. Or they might be deceitful, in which case, you need to know ahead of tim; before you decide to do any business with them!

Chapter Summary

- Unfortunately, the communication process is not as simple as puttin; words together in a coherent framework, and having someone els; hear and understand them!

- Language, both verbal and nonverbal, is subject to misinterpretatio; due to a variety of factors including culture, work hierarchy; shortcuts, and previous encounters with the listener(s).

- Nonverbal communication includes touch, visual cues like facial an; body expressions, tone of voice, and time and space (comfort zone);

- Body language may enhance the verbal language by repeating; complementing, or accenting it. It can alternatively detract from verbal language if what's being said by the body isn't the same a what's being said with the words.

28

Now that you recognize the importance of body language, Chapter hree brings practical applications for your newfound knowledge.

CHAPTER THREE

When Body Talks and What It Means

'here are plenty of signs that another person may nonverbally send you. ome are more obvious than others. When you're not confident in reading ther people's body language, keep it simple and look at the big picture. 'ou don't want to spend so much time trying to look for little signals that ou miss what they're actually saying and the overall message they're ending! Read the big gestures, not the little ones. As long as you're paying ttention, you'll know if they're bored or engaged.

Have you ever tried to do something, started overthinking it, and then ompletely lost your way? That's pretty common. Dancers, for example, ave a lot of muscle memory. Beginning dancers often find that they get ito their groove. However, as soon as they start thinking about the steps, ieir feet seem to get all tangled up. This is the Law of Reverse Effect, when ou try to force your conscious mind to take over something that your ubconscious usually handles.

The small signals from another person's body language are decoded by our subconscious. Once you start thinking about and looking for them, ou'll start to see little signs everywhere and be more likely to mistake an mocuous twitch for a subtle signal.

Let your subconscious handle the small stuff. Some of the nerve discussed in the previous chapter are actually found in your digestiv system. So yes, gut instinct is actually backed by science (sometimes)!

Preparing to read body language

Don't overthink it! Fortunately, to have a solid working knowledge o body language and how to interpret messages, you don't need to get to analytical. Consider the larger picture and look for the obvious signals smiles (or a lack thereof), arm and leg placement, what the hands are doing Just a quick scan can get you the information you're looking for. Speed reading the big signs is often enough to get you to your goals.

It does help if you're relaxed when you're attempting to read other people. Even if the situation is tense, you need to be calm and in control. B comfortable with discomfort, in other words. Mindful breathing an relaxation techniques can help you with this mindset, but long meditatio sessions aren't necessary (which is a good thing because you won't alway have time!).

When your brain senses that you're under threat or you feel anxious, th hormones and neurotransmitters mentioned in Chapter One spring int action. To reverse the heart-pounding and other effects of your fight-or flight response, try a simple breathing exercise. Breathe in for three counts hold for three, exhale for three. Do this three times. Another way to caln yourself is to try "box breathing" a few times. Inhale for three or fou counts, hold for three or four counts, exhale three or four, hold three or fou counts, and repeat.

Breathing relaxation methods are especially helpful when you're in ublic. They probably won't even be noticed by anyone else. You might so do these exercises backstage or out of sight before you do your power oses to feel more confident. (I will talk about these in detail in future hapters. Appearing confident, whether you feel it or not, is important in a umber of situations.)

Make sure that your emotions aren't affecting how you read others! eeling particularly stressed, bored, or defensive might cloud your own ninking. You might not be able to express yourself in the way that you ant, and you might not interpret what someone else is saying in the way nat they intend. In addition, the other person might pick up on this too, and hange their own language.

ontext is important

When reading others, bear in mind that body language always has to be ut in context. For example, I previously noted that tightly crossed arms ver your torso show anger or defensiveness. However, this behavior is also omething people do when they're cold. If you're in an igloo talking to omeone, they may not be angry or defensive. They may simply have nsufficiently warm clothing!

The other person's physique also should be taken into account. They night not be slumping as the result of an emotion but have back pain or aturally slumping shoulders. Maintaining eye contact isn't necessarily the ign of a liar, especially if the other person has a social anxiety disorder. hey may simply find eye contact extremely uncomfortable, for reasons nat have nothing to do with your conversation. People with arthritic hands may not squeeze your hand as firmly when they shake it.

By contrast, other people might need a gentle nudge to push themselves out of their comfort zone. If they're the poker-faced type, you need to catch them off guard for them to let the "mask" slip off. People who are feeling shy and defensive may hold an item like a notebook in front of them as shield. You can offer them a drink, ask them to hold something, or suggest some other action that uncurls their body.

All this being said, there are more obvious signals that you can pick up on pretty quickly. You can look for them without being creepy and understand what they mean. They're pretty common across different cultures and areas of the world and will help you determine what the other person's actual message is.

Eight common body language codes you can decipher

1. **Eyes**

   Did you know that people commonly look up and to the left when they're remembering something? And up and to the right when they're using their imaginations? If the other person is looking up to (their) right, they could be lying. Sometimes blinking too much indicates deceit too. And not looking at you in the eye, especially if they're looking to the side, might also indicate to you that they're not telling the truth.

   Not looking you in the eye can also mean boredom. If they're looking down during your conversation, they could be nervous or submissive.

34

Think about the last time you spoke to someone who didn't make a lot of eye contact with you. What kind of impression did you get? Probably not that they were confident or excited to talk to you!

Someone who actually does want to speak to you might have dilated pupils as a result of the attention chemicals in the body. This one's a little harder to see than some of the other clues! Don't spend too much time staring into the other's eyes to determine if their pupils are getting bigger or not. Take a look at some of the other signals they're sending instead.

2. Face

The eyes may be the window to the soul, but the smile is a window to the mood. Are they smiling? Is it genuine? If so, a happy person who is engaging with you. A slight smile combined with slightly raised eyebrows means the person is feeling friendly and not anxious about it.

A tight smile or half-smile, however, is the opposite signal. They may be bored, irritated, unsure, or something else. Definitely not happy and engaged. Keep in mind, their expression or mood may have nothing to do with you, so don't take it personally if their smile is tight and fake.

Lips tight and pursed together? Also not a happy person. Relaxed lips and mouth show a positive mood. In fact, relaxed facial features and muscles are generally positive signals. Think about what you do when you get stressed out. Clench your jaw? Grind your teeth?

Tense your shoulders and hunch them around your ears? Mos people don't react to stress by relaxing. They react by tensing an clenching.

If the other person is touching their mouth or covering it as they talk they very well might be lying to you. It's their subconscious shinin, through and trying to prevent false words from slipping out. (O they might be in the middle of eating and don't want to spit food a you accidentally. Context!)

3. How physically close they are

This particular clue, as noted in Chapter One, is definitely affecte by culture. Different cultures have different social guidelines.

However, subject to that caveat, people who want to engage wit you or are feeling positive about you will be closer to you. Whe you're with your good friends, do you tend to sit closer to them tha you would to someone you don't know? Or farther away?

If you approach another person and they pull away, that's a goo indicator that they're not feeling great about chatting with you Someone who's standing a good distance from you may be naturall shy or a bit reserved. Look for more clues to see if they really don want to talk to you personally or if they're just a bit standoffish wit people they don't know.

4. Whether they're mirroring you

It's natural for humans to reflect the gestures of someone they car about or want to get to know better. If you lean an elbow on the tabl

36

and the other person does too within a few seconds, they're mirroring. Sip your drink. Did they pick up their drink too?

We'll get into this more in future chapters, but mirroring someone is a good way to get them to like and trust you.

5. Head and neck movement

Ever been in a class or meeting where the presenter droned on and on and on? Did you feel yourself nodding your head faster, desperate to get that person to wind it up or stop talking?

Right. A slower nod means more patience. The person is interested in what you have to say. They're not frantically trying to get you to shut up, but they're showing you that they get it. They might also tilt their head a bit to the side to show interest.

Not moving the head at all when speaking is a sign of being very serious, or having authority. When you're a bobblehead, people will take you about as seriously as they will a bobblehead figurine. Too much movement looks nervous, not confident.

You've probably been in a situation where you were talking with your colleagues while waiting for a meeting to start. What happened when the boss walked in? People stopped talking to pay attention. Those with less power are looked at less often. To determine the most important person in the room, find who everyone's looking at.

By contrast, if someone's leaning their head back, away from you, they're uncertain or suspicious.

Rapid swallowing is often a sign of fear or embarrassment. A hand to the throat is often someone trying to hide this. Very simply people who make motions to conceal or cover up something are likely hiding something! That's the subconscious speaking.

6. Legs and feet

Looking at the position of a person's feet is a great way to see how they are really feeling! Many of us control our faces and gestures but don't pay as much attention to the feet.

Where are the other person's feet pointing? If it's toward you, then they likely do want to connect with you. Interested and engaged people are turned toward you with their feet and their faces. If their feet are pointing away from you, they want to head in some other direction, toward another person, the exit, or wherever they're aiming their feet. You don't have to spend too long looking down at the floor. A quick glance should tell you whether they're interested or not.

Maybe as you look down, you see the other person's feet angled inwards or curled around either themselves or a chair leg. Does that seem like confident body language to you? Probably not. These are signs the individual you're studying is feeling awkward or anxious.

Someone's posture or how they stand is also a good indicator of their true emotions. A relaxed stance with legs shoulder-width apart shows you a confident, relaxed person, or at least, someone who is trying to appear so!

Having legs and feet together signals anxiety. The person is trying to make themselves smaller. Similarly, having crossed legs or feet is another attempt to appear smaller. A confident person will take up space.

7. Hands

When making hand gestures, people tend to aim towards someone they feel they have a relationship with. These movements may also include elbows, depending on the position. Pointing fingers is considered rude, at least in the United States. But your hands are usually in the direction of the person you're interested in just as your feet are.

Hands are also used to make gestures when people are talking. Open, sweeping gestures are usually found in people who are confident in themselves and what they're saying.

When sitting down and resting their head or chin on one hand, a person is showing interest in what the other person is saying.

Negative or unfavorable gestures are likewise pretty clear. Keeping hands in pockets or on the head indicates nervousness or deceitfulness. Sitting with their head in both hands usually signals boredom.

Someone who holds an item like a folio or a purse in front of their chest as a shield while talking is defending themselves from the other person. This is a pretty clear gesture. Many times, it has nothing to do with the person they're defending themselves against!

It's more of a sign that they're nervous or feeling defensive i general.

8. Arms

Crossed arms, as mentioned previously, can signal anger an defensiveness but also anxiety or being closed off. However, whe the crossed arms are paired with a relaxed and confident body, the can actually signal a positive attitude.

Hands on hips is asserting dominance, at least when done in publi Standing with legs spread wide and hands on hips is also a powe pose that makes many individuals feel more confident, especiall when they're about to do something like give a presentation to a bi audience.

Reading body language by mood

There are plenty of gestures and expressions that you can look for whe trying to understand another person's nonverbal communication. As yo saw above, different parts of the body can be involved in a conversation i varying ways.

This means that reading other people's body language is not an exac science. There are general clues to what someone is saying with their body but these gestures and positions may be interpreted differently dependin on whether they come from a different background or whether they have disorder or physical issue that changes their body language.

Many times, the way to resolve apparent contradictions is to see if mos of the cues are leading in one direction or the other. If most of th xpressions are those of someone who's relaxed and happy, then an xpression that normally indicates tension and anxiety is likely due to utside influences such as the weather.

This method works in the other direction as well. Imagine someone ho's slumped, clenching their hands, and staring at the ground, but has 1eir feet pointed in your direction. Are they likely to be enthusiastically ngaging with you? No, the feet are probably just a coincidence.

Below are common body language signals for different types of moods nd emotions.

1. Happy/positive/engaged

When people are feeling positive, they tend to carry themselves with good posture. Arms, legs, and hands are relaxed. Their body is open to you, not crossed or blocked off. They may be smiling—a genuine smile, not a half-baked one. They will make regular eye contact with you, but not stare awkwardly.

If they want to hear more from you and are engaged with you, they will likely stand closer. They may nod slowly as they take in what you're saying or tilt their heads a bit to the side. If they're sitting down, they may prop their head up on one elbow.

In general, their hands, elbows, and feet will be pointed towards you. They'll reflect back or mirror gestures that you make. If you can see their pupils, they will be dilated.

When you take a sip of water, they will too. People who want to engage with you will reflect your gestures.

41

2. Deceitful

Someone who's lying has difficulty looking you in the eye. The may be looking up and to the right or blinking too often.

When speaking, they may touch their lips or cover their mouths Alternatively, they might put their hands in their pockets out o sight.

If their body language is about hiding or covering, it's very likel that they are not being truthful with you.

3. Awkward/anxious/nervous

These people are not looking you in the eye, either. They may cur their feet around themselves or a chair leg if they're sitting down They also might be blinking a lot or swallowing too often. A anxious person stands with their legs squeezed together. Their arm may also be crossed in the interest of making themselves physicall smaller.

You might also notice that they're slouched. Usually, their bodie aren't open towards you. They're holding something in front o them to ward you, and probably other people, off or away fron them.

Someone who's feeling anxious is also likely to look pretty tense— clenched jaws, clenched hands, tight mouths. They might be lookin around the room, scanning for threats. They're not particularl focused on you (unless they find you a threat in some way).

4. Negative (or at least not favorable) towards you personally

If they're nodding their heads rapidly, you should probably take a break from talking! Take a look at their feet. If their feet are pointed away from you, they'd probably rather be somewhere else. And if they're seated with both hands supporting their head, they're bored.

If they're smiling, it won't be a real smile, but a tight or fake one. Their lips may be pressed together. They're not mimicking your gestures. Regarding eye contact, they may not even look at you in the first place.

tep-by-step body scan

So far, I've taken all these indicators and clues piece by piece—first by ody part, and then by mood. How do you put them all together? In order) "speed-read" someone else, recall that it's the larger movements and xpressions that will give you a quick overview of what the other person is ·ying to tell you.

1. Overall posture

When you take in another person as a whole, what is the impression you get? Are they standing tall and relaxed? Or are they hunched over and slouching? Can you see if their muscles are clenched? Do they seem to be making themselves smaller? Or are they taking up a reasonable amount of space? If they're making gestures of some kind, are the movements small and constrained, or are they more open?

2. Face

The first thing you look for, because it's a major indicator, is a smile. If they have one, is it genuine? As you start talking to them, are they making eye contact with you? Are they nodding as you speak, taking in what you're saying? Or are they nodding vigorously, their eyes darting around the room? Is their face relaxed or their jaw clenched?

3. Arms, legs, hands, feet

Are they open or relaxed? Facing in your direction?

Or are they twisted, crossed, clenched, or squeezed? Are they hidden or aimed at someone or something else in the room?

Case study

Imagine you're in an office observing two people, Pat and Chris, who stand facing each other.

Pat is standing straight, with legs about shoulder-width apart, nodding slowly at what Chris is saying. Pat's feet are pointed at Chris. Her hands are relaxed and open. There's a faint but real smile on Pat's face as she looks directly at Chris.

Chris stands with his legs close together, and he is holding his folio close to his chest. His feet are pointed a little bit inwards at each other. He's mostly looking at Pat, but every so often, his gaze drifts off in a different direction. He's not smiling, and when he's not talking, he presses his lips together.

What do you conclude as a result of your observations?

Pat is confident in herself, and she's also interested in what Chris is aying. He's a bit defensive and feeling nervous.

What's the relationship between the two? Because Pat is not asserting ominance, she is either not his boss, or she is his superior but trying to put im at ease. He might be new, or he may just be a nervous person in general.

Speed-reading is an exercise you can do pretty much anywhere you see ther people. Try it on your morning commute, the coffee shop, your ompany's cafeteria, or even a networking event. Study the way people hold 1emselves. How does their body language come across to you? If you see vo people talking, try to figure out what their relationship is.

Chapter Summary

- Our subconscious, or gut instinct, does a lot of the work in reading body language for us, particularly with the small movements that most of us make unconsciously.

- We don't need to overthink someone else's nonverbal communication or spend too much time analyzing it.

- There are some larger gestures and obvious cues that we can read to understand how someone else is feeling or what they're trying to tell us.

- Different body parts have varying ways of expressing nonverbal messages.

- In general, open and relaxed postures, faces, and gestures indicat positive emotions and interest.

- By contrast, those squeezing themselves together to look small o showing obvious tension are not at ease and may need some specia handling.

In the next chapter, you will learn how to develop winning bod language for a great personality!

CHAPTER FOUR

How to Develop a Winning Personality With Your Body Language

ou can project confidence and interest. (More details in the last chapter, if ou haven't had a chance to get there yet!) By learning about how others ommunicate nonverbally, you now know some of the gestures and postures 1at you can use when you're in front of other people.

But you want to be successful! That requires more than just smiling hen you're speaking to someone. In fact, smiling too much can have a egative effect, making you look nervous or less confident.

Think about people you admire and want to listen to. You don't have to now them. Maybe they're on TV, or you've seen them on the Internet. Iow do they come across? Do they seem insecure or nervous? When ıey're being interviewed, does the interviewer's gaze wander? If the erson being interviewed is charismatic and appealing, you'll notice the ıterviewer stays locked on their guest unless they're turning to the audience) make a point.

Or maybe you've observed people at the office. When you're in a ıeeting and the people in charge aren't there yet, you and your colleagues probably chat among yourselves or play on your phones. But what happen when the CEO or manager walks into the room? Everyone looks at them sets down the phone, and wraps the conversation they're having with thei neighbor. Look at the person in charge. Does that person fidget, seen anxious, or appear defensive? Or do they walk in like they own the place?

Have you been to a comedy show lately? Do you laugh harder with comic who knows they're funny or the one who looks relieved if someon chuckles during their set?

Human beings prefer to follow leaders who seem confident. Think abou who you want to pay attention to, and who seems to draw your focu naturally. Do you want to listen to someone who seems unsure o themselves or avoids your eyes when they talk to you?

No matter how the leader is feeling at that moment in time, they need t be seen as secure in themselves. No defensive, anxious, or nervous bod language will be displayed. If they do, they lose the audience. To hav power, others must acknowledge that person's power. And if they displa weakness in one way or another, they'll lose power.

Maybe you're feeling unsure of yourself right now. Body language ma be new to you, and you recognized your body in the descriptions of thos who are defensive, anxious, or negative. That's okay. You don't actuall have to be self-confident to act like you are! And as a bonus, the more self assured you act, the more confident you'll actually be. It's a positiv feedback loop. If you act confident and feel confident, others will respon to your confidence, making you feel more confident.

What else do you need to consider when you want to project onfidence? You can condition yourself to act with more assurance. ortunately, we're in the age of the internet, so there are plenty of videos of uccessful people like Richard Branson, Steve Jobs, and Mark Cuban. Want) be more confident? Study their body language and copy it. Practice these 1oves and bolster your own confidence.

ody language of the "Winner's Club"

How about the fist bump? Germaphobes prefer this to a handshake, as ichard Branson does. It says you're a little unconventional and not too todgy. Or, consider a double thumbs-up, which is what Jack Ma of Alibaba 1 Chinese company similar to Amazon in the US) likes to use. It has onnotations with Buddha in China but also sends a positive message to mericans.

I mentioned mirroring in the last chapter, which is something you often ee Mark Zuckerberg doing. Interestingly, if you mirror someone else, you ecome more empathetic and are more likely to understand the other erson's message.

Sheryl Sandberg tends to lean towards her audience or whomever she's peaking to. She tilts and pushes her head forward in a controlled manner. 'his shows her listeners that she has lots of ideas and is interested in ngaging with them.

There's more about public speaking in the next chapter, but what made teve Jobs so effective was that he actually made eye contact with his udience. It's very powerful when audience members feel that you're speaking to them personally.

The go-to move for Mark Cuban is a genuine smile. It conveys warmth but can also command respect when paired with authoritative bod language such as big gestures.

Angela Merkel, the Chancellor of Germany, is known for "steepling her fingers. You don't have to sit down to do this because it works whil you're standing up too. Hold your hands in a triangle, with the fingertip just touching. This position is also great if you have trouble with what to d with your hands when you're not gesturing!

Notice that all these gestures are pretty natural. None of them are strang contortions that you have to practice in the mirror for weeks to get righ You might even be doing some of them already. In other words, using bod language effectively and successfully doesn't have to be difficult c unnatural.

In addition, these motions all convey warmth. You're not coming off a stern or unapproachable, because that doesn't make you likable. You don' have to be a taskmaster or a robot to deliver an effective message. In fac being a robot will make you less effective! Being confident and having good personality mean that you're seen as trustworthy, open, and friendly That is the kind of person that other people want to get to know, connect to and be influenced by.

Nine ways to command (positive) attention

All of the people mentioned above are known for their physica presence. Others pay attention to them when they're speaking, partl ecause they're powerful people who have influence in their fields, but also ue to the confident body language they use while in public. Here are six ays to bring attention to yourself so that people can engage with your essage.

Many of these tips are based on being or appearing confident. People on't pay much attention to someone who isn't confident. They'd rather ear from a person who is, even if that person doesn't really know what ey're talking about! As long as the person is faking it well enough, others ill believe it.

1. Meet in the other's space for a firm handshake

Don't wait for the other person to shake your hand. Step forward and offer yours first, as the sign of a person confident in themselves.

When it comes to the handshake, no limp hands! Firmly grasp the other's hand, but not so firmly that it's painful or crushing. Shake up and down a few times with eye contact and then release. If you're concerned about whether your handshake is too delicate or too strong, ask friends and colleagues to give you some feedback.

2. Don't move too much

Animals under threat often duck their heads in small movements. Their eyes dart around, seeking escape. Well, we're animals too, and the same goes for us.

If you move your head a lot when speaking, you'll look powerless. Keeping your head still conveys seriousness and a sense of authority. This is especially true for women, who are often seen as less serious due to their gender.

Stop fidgeting. Yes, just like your mother told you! People fidget i various manners, but all of it needs to end. Twirling your hai shaking your feet, playing with your hands and fingers, touchin your face or neck as you speak—all of these make you look anxiou You may need to practice sitting and standing still!

Try poses and postures that don't allow you to fidget, especiall those that are power signals in and of themselves. For exampl steepling your fingers is a sign of authority and confidence. But i happens to keep your fingers from fidgeting around your face, neck or hair as well.

As with many of the body language signals I discuss, there's positive impact when you do something, but a negative impact i you do too much of it. For example, people who frequently use arr and hand gestures come across in a more positive way than peopl who do not. However, once the gestures get too frenetic, or they'r happening in the air above your shoulders, it's no longe authoritative. These gestures make you look out of control, an therefore less powerful.

In short, some movements are beneficial and will make you mor confident and likable, but they must be controlled to have a positive impac You need to look like you're consciously making a choice to make th movement, whatever it is, not allowing yourself to flail or move too much

3. Fake it 'til you make it

Fakery doesn't work for everything. For example, if you're fearful, you won't easily be able to pretend that you're not. Your body language will leak clues that you're afraid.

In contrast, taking on confident stances such as power poses, postures, and gestures often gets the point across. Not only does it send the message to others that you're confident, it helps you send that signal to yourself! Over time, as your confidence grows, these gestures will be more authentic.

Power poses include standing with arms and legs apart. This makes you look bigger, instead of small and fearful. It's the Superman stance. Putting your feet up on the desk may not always be advisable, depending on who's on the other side of it, but it is a power pose as well.

Dressing for success is an actual concept, though not in the sense of whether you should or should not wear a suit. (That depends entirely on your field.) The more confident you feel in your clothes, the more self-assured you'll be.

Therefore, don't wear anything that pulls or tugs or needs constant adjustment. Fiddling with your clothes makes you look nervous. Wear something that you know you look good in and that you can stand or sit in while wearing. As they say, dress for the job you want, not the job you have. Let your clothes communicate confidently too.

And if you're going to fake it, fake it properly. (Who knew there

was a right way and a wrong way to fake it?) In other words, mak
sure you're using gestures and power poses thoughtfully.

It's often a bad idea to point your finger. Some may think
expresses dominance, but most people read it either as annoyin
parental control, or bullying. Remember that the secret to a winnin
body language is likeability and confidence. No one likes a bully.

4. Watch your palms

There is meaning to whether your palms are facing up or facin
down. Palms down is the more confident posture. Whether seated a
a desk or standing to give a presentation, not showing your palm
signals confidence and authority. In fact, if you're behind a desk
you may need to occasionally turn them upward, so you don't com
off as overbearing!

Palms up indicates less power. You may notice when others ar
presenting their thoughts, their palms are up, asking for acceptance
Palms down is more control over the conversation.

However, in some instances, you may want to have your palms up
even though it is more supplicative. Depending on th
circumstances, such a gesture helps convey that you're trustworthy

Either way, when shaking someone else's hand, keep your palm dry
A sweaty palm is definitely not a friendly palm!

Maintaining relaxed hands and palms is important as well
Clenching your fists indicates anger. Gripping an object, such as
purse or notepad, too tightly, betrays nervousness. If you can't hol

them loosely, set them down. Doing so will also help you avoid using the item as a shield between you and other people.

Hiding your hands, maybe behind your back or in your pockets, suggests to others that you're hiding something. You want to come across as open, so make sure that wherever you place your palms, it's in full view of whomever you're speaking to.

When sitting down, steepling your fingers together a la Angela Merkel is a welcoming yet confident gesture. Try it!

People trust those who "talk with their hands," so don't be shy about using them. Before we had words, we had nonverbal communication, and hands are an important part of it. When you show your hands, you seem trustworthy

5. Pinch your thumb and forefinger together

This gesture is especially effective when you want to emphasize a specific point that you're making. Use it sparingly, and you'll convey authority and confidence. If you use it too frequently, it just looks …weird.

6. Raise those eyebrows

This gesture indicates you're open. People feeling vulnerable are often closed off and defensive, so showing openness is a sign of confidence. Turning your head slowly and then raising your eyebrows as you look at someone is a command for attention. Think of Roger Moore's James Bond character for inspiration.

7. Stand (or sit) up straight

Yes, just like your mom told you. Hold your head high and shoulder back. Good posture is not just a pose of confidence and authority. I helps prevent unnecessary back and neck pain and allows for prope breathing. Believe it or not, that's important for self-assurance too If you're not breathing properly, you'll probably be tense, and you voice will come out higher than normal. Relaxed breathing i confident breathing.

When sitting, your back should still be straight, with your feet fla on the floor. If you're shorter, there may be times when the availabl seats won't let you plant your feet. In that situation, you may choos to stand, especially if the alternative is letting your feet dangle lik a child's. When you're in your own space, you may want a footres to avoid the problem.

Take up space. Avoid making yourself look small, which reads a completely powerless and vulnerable. Arms and legs should not b crossed as that makes you smaller. Hunching over or pulling inwar in any way is a powerless posture, as is holding your hands in th classic fig-leaf position in front of your crotch. Let your arms be a your sides, not your middle.

This is another important tip for women, who, in many cultures, ar expected to be less powerful or to defer to men. Women leaders mus display confidence just as their male counterparts do. You don' want to spread your legs so wide that you're sprawling, of course But there's no reason to cross your legs or hold your arms close t your torso. If you are sitting behind a desk or table, spread the materials out. If you're standing, legs should be at least shoulder-width, and possibly hip-width, apart. Plant feet firmly on the floor.

Although putting your hands on your hips takes up space, other people find it too aggressive. Avoid standing with your arms akimbo. Try steepling or using more gestures with your hands and arms.

8. Facial expressions, including your smile

Your mom probably told you to smile too, and for a good reason. Smiling helps you appear trustworthy, which means people will pay attention to and engage with you. Like power poses, smiles have a feedback loop; smiling makes you happier.

Smiling is the go-to power move for some powerful people. A genuine smile is open and displays your trustworthiness and likeability. It's warm and an indicator of interest in the other person.

Try not to yawn in someone else's face! You can't signify boredom any more clearly, even if your yawn is due to something else.

9. Eye contact

This doesn't mean staring into the other person's eyes like you're trying to suck their soul out of them. But you also need to avoid looking away or down for too long, which are fearful and avoidant gestures. Confident people look the other person directly in the eye. Don't let your eyes flit from person to person or around the room if you're in the middle of a conversation. You'll seem bored and uninterested.

Do you wear eyeglasses? If so, looking at other people over the rir of your specs conveys contempt, especially if doing so causes yo to look down at them. Looking through your glasses instead of ove them makes you appear friendly and open.

If you're indoors, don't wear your sunglasses. Because people can see your eyes, you look like you're trying to hide something.

Having a likable personality is easy to develop through your bod language. Before even opening your mouth, you can command th attention of other people. And best of all, even if you don't fee particularly confident right now, you can work on your seli assurance by using the techniques mentioned above.

Confidence is not the same as arrogance. Being self-assured doe not mean being self-absorbed or feeling superior. Those things ar not particularly likable! A winning personality is open, friendly, an trustworthy.

One more thing to be aware of is phone etiquette. It's helpful at a times, but especially when talking to someone who grew up befor the era of the smartphone. If you're looking at or fidgeting with you phone while someone's talking, you come across as ver disrespectful. Whether or not you mean to be, that is what your bod language is saying.

If you want to be respected by others, you also need to show ther respect. People don't look up to someone who calls themselves leader but is rude and demeans or ignores others. Good phone etiquette is essential. If you're in the middle of a conversation, you don't need to look at or answer your phone (unless you're a first responder). Taking calls while you're surrounded by other people is also rude.

The best way to show your interest in someone else is to stay in the onversation with them—not looking around the room, looking at the floor, r checking the phone every time someone likes your Instagram post. It's ot checking your email every two seconds, but engaging with the other erson, being genuinely interested in them, smiling and making eye contact. Vhen you do that, your audience will leave thinking you have a great ersonality!

Using the language of self-confidence is the language of successful, harismatic individuals. And you can learn this language by using the echniques mentioned above.

Chapter Summary

- Watching successful people interact is a good way to find how others project confidence.

- To improve your confidence, watch powerful and successful people on TV or online, and mimic what they do as much as you can.

- Confidence is a characteristic that you can learn, and faking confidence actually leads to having it.

- Certain gestures, such as a firm handshake and controlled arm movements, make you appear more confident, as will smiling and making more eye contact.

- Practice confident body language to command the attention of others

In the next chapter, I will discuss using nonverbal communication for good public speaking. Assure yourself and your audience that you know what you're talking about, and listening to you will be worth their while.

CHAPTER FIVE

Public Speaking and Presentations

What's the most important aspect of nonverbal communication when you're speaking in public? Projecting confidence! Audiences want to hear experts, so you need to carry yourself like one, whether you're feeling self-assured or not. Fortunately, confidence is something that you can fake, and acting confident in itself will help you be confident! There's more detail in Chapter Four about the positive feedback loop of confidence if you haven't had a chance to get to it yet.

Many people get nervous about speaking in front of people, especially in their initial engagements. So, in addition to the nonverbal communication, I will talk more about in this chapter, there are a few things you need to do to prepare a talk. First, know what your key points are. Trying to memorize or read a speech leads to bad body language, so avoid it. And make sure you rehearse your talk beforehand. How long did it take you? Make sure it fits into the time allotted to you.

Prepping will help you feel more confident. There are other ways you can use your body language to become an effective public speaker and presenter.

Entering the room

You've probably heard that you never get a second chance to make first impression. It seems a bit cliché, but it's true. Your public presentatio begins the minute you're in public! If anyone watches you enter, they nee to see self-assurance right away.

Any time you're in front of an audience, it's important to stand tall an with good posture. Slouching won't win you any respect. While you'r standing, plant your weight on both feet. This will help you stand still an avoid fidgeting, which makes you look nervous. Remember that exces movement gives off the impression of being weak and powerless, which i exactly what people listening to you don't want to see.

Avoid shuffling as you walk. It makes you look like you don't knov where you're going! Pick up your feet as you go, with a deliberate stride Here's another fake it 'til you make it tip: Look like you know where you'r going. It doesn't matter whether you do or not; you just need to create tha impression.

Just as it's better to avoid looking down when you're speaking t someone face to face, don't look down as you're entering a room eithei Keep your head and eyes up, which is a good way to command respect. A the same time, swaggering is also a bad idea. You'll seem cocky instead o confident. And don't be rude! Avoid stepping on toes and bumping int others.

Prepping and beginning the presentation

Use the same confident strides to walk toward the podium, or whereve

62

ou'll be speaking. Before you start talking, give yourself and the audience moment to settle. Settle your weight equally on both feet. Make some eye ontact with audience members. Take some deep breaths to soothe your ystem so your nerves don't get the better of you.

When you first start giving presentations, you might feel safer staying ehind the podium. You can place your hands on it to avoid fidgeting, specially if you're the kind of person who moves around a lot when they're ervous. Standing solidly in one spot might help you feel grounded. Plus, very time you take even a quick glance down, you'll have your notes right here.

However, audiences like it when you remove the shield or barrier etween you by moving around the stage, out from behind the podium. A uirk of human nature is that we tend to like people who are physically loser to us. So approach your audience, particularly if you've given your lk a few times, and you know it pretty well. You might emphasize a certain oint by stepping towards the audience to deliver it, and then move back to here you started from.

When you're moving, don't deliver your key concepts. Save those for hen you come to a stop close to the people listening. Remember that tillness conveys authority, so being solidly planted in one spot will help ue audience focus on your words. Complete the thought or idea before you literally) move on.

Gestures also help you underline important parts in your talk. Using novements natural to any anecdotes you're telling makes you look more onfident. Discussing something rising? Swoop your arm up, but not above

63

your shoulders. If you're not sure what looks natural or fits with your talk search online for someone who talks about your subject. Watch their presentations. Do the gestures look natural? Do they help clarify the topic If so, practice them.

As with many body language communications, you need to strike balance. Gesture, but not too much! Only do so enough to signify expertise If you overdo it, you look nervous and unsure. Shifting your weight touching your face/hair/neck, and repeatedly clicking your pen are all nervous gestures. While you don't want to be so still that the audienc mistakes you for a robot or automation, you don't want to make so many gestures that you look erratic and untrustworthy either. Choose your movements with restraint.

Suppose you've watched some videos and know the main points you'd like to include. How do you add gestures into your speech? As you're writing out your talk, or the outline of it (since effective speeches are usually not scripted word-for-word), look for places where movement would add to the presentation.

Where did the person you watched use movement to improve their talk Do you have any anecdotes or stories that could use some gestures? What are the important points you want the audience to take away from your talk Reinforce those points with some body language.

Knowing which movements you want to keep will help your speech pack more of a punch. There's a bonus, too! It'll give you some idea of what to do with your hands as you're speaking. Clasping them like you're holding fig leaves in front of your crotch makes you look pretty much the opposit

64

f confident! If you're using your hands and arms for movement, they don't ave a chance to sneak down there.

Feel your presentation as you're developing it. When Brene Brown peaks, she often gestures toward her heart, which is a way to be earnest nd suggest that's where she's speaking from.

People make decisions based on emotions and then justify them with icts afterward. If you can make your audience feel something, they'll be 1ore engaged. It will also help you be more confident about your speech.

What emotions link you with the subject matter? What emotions do you /ant your audience to feel? How can you use body language to express it? 'ou might want to go back and watch the speaker on your subject again, to ive you some ideas. The more your audience is emotionally tied to the resentation, the more likely they are to respond the way you want.

You rehearse your words, right? Do the same for your movements. ractice your talk with the movements that you think will make your talk 1ore powerful and engaging. You can rehearse in front of a mirror, or :cord it and play it back later. Do the visuals match the verbal language? re there more places where you can use gestures? Effective speakers use 1ore movement in their talks than less effective ones do. Add in more if 1ey improve the clarity or impact of your words.

ssential body language to own the stage

Once you've rehearsed your speech and decided on your gestures, make ure that you're engaging with the audience when you deliver your talk. hey've come to hear (and see) you. They're taking time out of their schedules, so make it worth their while. Keep them interested in what you'r' saying. Make sure their attention on you, not on their phones or the tree outside the window.

How can you do that? Once again, body language saves the day! Whe you're using it and maximizing its power, people will be drawn to you.

Have you ever had to sit through a presentation given by a really du presenter? Did you listen to them the whole time, or tune them out at som point? Did you keep your eyes on them, or did you end up staring out th window, or doodling in your notebook, or playing games on your phone Did you wish really hard that you were anywhere else but there? It probabl felt like a complete waste of time, even if the material was interesting o relevant.

Don't be that dull presenter. It's likely they read off their notes th whole time. Maybe even in a droning monotone. They didn't look up at yo at all. Maybe they even read their slides word-for-word.

It's possible they were so boring that you couldn't remember their nam afterward. Or you made a note of it, so you knew never to attend one of thei sessions again! Could you remember any of the points they made? Did yo even hear any of the points they made or were you completely tuned ou after a few minutes?

Right! Think about what they did...and do the opposite. Here are si: ways to use your nonverbal communication skills to improve your publi speaking. Whether you're giving a presentation or a talk, these suggestion will help you make the impact you're looking for.

1. Find an appropriate level of nervous energy

You're probably not going to be perfectly calm. Even experienced speakers have some nervousness before they go on stage or deliver a presentation. Having some energy is actually good for your presentation. A little stress is good. Those neurotransmitters and hormones from Chapter One also help you focus and get clarity, in addition to increasing your heart rate and blood flow.

Too much stress? You'll be jittering all over the place and displaying plenty of nervous body language. Balance!

Try taking deep breaths that reach all the way to your stomach. Let them out slowly as well. You can combine the breaths with tensing your muscles too. For example, clench your fists on the inhale, and allow your hands to relax and hang loosely on the exhale. When you relax clenched muscles, it makes your brain think you're relaxed. Then, the chemicals behind the anxiety signals will decrease as well.

Stress relievers are best done backstage, or at least out of sight of your audience. Remember, you're looking to appear calm, cool, collected, and likable. They don't need to see you struggling with your nervousness.

2. Avoid showing the audience your back

Humans are very attuned to faces. This is how we get information about people. In fact, our brains are so used to looking for faces that you might see them in inanimate objects like the moon, fruit, or toast. (This effect is known as *pareidolia*.)

Our fascination with faces is also why people who run or walk i the road should run facing traffic and not with traffic as cyclists do People are more likely to see your face, recognize that you're person, and try to avoid hitting you!

Faces and facial expressions are an important part c communication. People read emotions not from the words anothe person says, but from their body language. If someone can't rea your expression, they may not understand or misinterpret th message you're trying to deliver. Your audience needs to be able t see your face when you talk, so they get what you're saying.

Turning away from the people you're speaking to breaks you connection with them as well. Have you ever felt engaged wit someone's back? Of course not, you connect with people whos faces you can see. Why are webinars and online video chats s popular? So the people on the call can see each other.

For the audience to be engaged in your talk, you need to connec with them. And for that to happen, they can't be looking at your bac or profile. They need to be seeing you full on.

3. Look up from your notes

Have you ever seen a presentation, either live or on video, with terrific speaker? Someone who commanded your attention, wh made sense? You couldn't look away from them. What did they do They probably didn't spend much time, if any, looking down at thei notes. They spoke to their audience. They made eye contact witl people in the room and interacted with those gathered in front of them.

If you're staring down at your notes, by definition, you're not interacting with the people who are there to listen to you. How do you engage with people? Not by looking away from them. Not by looking down at the podium in front of you.

In addition, when you're not looking up, you don't look confident. If you keep your eyes on your notes the whole time, it'll seem like you have to do that because you don't know your material. By contrast, someone who barely looks at their notes, if at all, clearly knows what they're talking about!

Know the important points you want to make. Write keywords and phrases on your notes to remind you of these points. That way, you can simply glance down at them occasionally to make sure you haven't forgotten anything while looking at your audience, so they feel as if you're knowledgeably speaking directly to them.

4. Look at audience members specifically, instead of letting your eyes roam over them

Keeping your eyes on the air above people's heads while you're speaking disconnects you from the audience. They can tell you're looking over them, not at them. Do you think that reads as confident? Nope! They'll take it as nervousness, which it very likely is.

Recall that you're there to be an expert in whatever you're talking about. Even if you don't feel confident, you need to look confiden Make eye contact with specific people in the audience. This is th act of a self-assured speaker who has mastered their material. Eve the listeners you're not looking at in that particular moment wi respect your knowledge.

Eye contact also makes a direct connection between you and th person you're looking at. While you may be the only one talking, feels more like a conversation than a monologue to that other person It gives them the impression that you know the struggles they'v been through, and the solution you're discussing was develope with that particular person in mind.

As with moving around the stage, maintain eye contact for an entir sentence or thought before moving on to the next person and idea Otherwise, the connection breaks, or the contact seems mor accidental than deliberate.

5. **Keep your body open to the audience and use the gestures you practiced**

When you appear defensive or closed off, it makes you look like yo don't want to be there, or that you don't agree with what you ar saying. Either way, it's not a positive message. It suggests you ar not confident in your message, and you don't want to engage wit your audience.

Even if the above is true, you still don't want to communicate tha to your listeners! Avoid crossing your arms or holding your notes a a barrier between you and the audience. It's another reason to step out from behind the podium as well. Now there's no shield between you and the audience. It's a vulnerable position, but when you do it on purpose, that shows confidence.

Move around. Watching someone stand perfectly still, whether they're behind a podium or not, is still boring! Approaching the audience will make you more likable, too. The closer you are to people, the more connected they feel to you and what you're saying. Obviously, you'll need to have a firm grip on your content, so you can leave your notes for a bit in order to engage.

When you step toward your listeners to deliver an important point, make sure you don't keep moving as you explain the point. Plant your feet firmly until you've made it. Then you can walk back to your starting position.

Using your gestures can make a strong impact, particularly if you're standing still. You've practiced these movements, so they are natural and occur appropriately during your talk. You're not raising your arm when talking about a decline in a statistical number, for example. If you naturally talk with your hands, as many people do, go for it. Your natural movements appear authentic.

The more appropriate movements you use during your talk, the better. Audiences rate speakers who use more gestures better than those who use fewer. As always, balance though! Waving your arms around for no apparent reason won't add to your speech but detract from it.

71

6. Avoid power poses *during* the presentation

I discussed the impact of these in the previous chapter. Adopting powerful pose makes you feel more confident, so you perform mor confidently. The more confident you are, the more people respon Therefore, if you're feeling nervous or in need of a little confidenc booster, you can pose and hold a few times backstage. C somewhere else where you're out of sight of the audience.

Why not in front of the audience? As I mentioned above, peopl don't want to see you trying to be more confident. They want to se a confident person the minute they see you.

In addition, they mostly look aggressive. Standing in the Superma position with legs spread wide and hands on your hips comes off a intimidating. As a speaker, you want the audience to respect you an your confidence. You don't want them to feel that you're trying t dominate or intimidate them.

An engaging presenter isn't trying to force the audience to d anything even if your speech includes a call-to-action, as most c them should. You want them to feel confident that you hav something to say that is valuable to them. That's why they shoul listen to you, not because you're intimidating them into takin action.

Charisma and body language

You've probably heard about charismatic people, and you might eve have met someone with a lot of charisma. Former U.S. President Bi 'linton was known for his charisma. When he spoke to you, no matter who ou were—a truck driver, a diner waitress, a political opponent—he made ou feel that you were the only person in the room.

The public generally enjoys listening to and learning from charismatic eople. Most find them easier to engage with than less charismatic people. ortunately, even if you're not sure that you have this characteristic at the 1oment, you can learn and practice it just as you're doing with body 1nguage.

How is charisma defined? It's the confluence of three factors: presence, ower, and warmth.

Presence is being in the moment. When you're talking to someone,)cus on them. As Clinton demonstrated, the person you're talking to is the 1ly person in the room at that moment. You're not looking at your phone, 1inking about your shoes, or looking to see if a more interesting person has 1tered the room. Being present is a way to show respect as well as a way ） connect. You can't engage with anyone, much less an audience, if your 1ind is elsewhere.

Power is the ability to influence others. Raw power is not engaging or kable. Raw power is the bully who can take your lunch money because 1ey're bigger than you. Without leavening it with presence or warmth, ower is domineering, aggressive, and confrontational. It's difficult to)nnect to. But the whole point of a presentation is to actually create a link 'ith your audience and put them in a position where they want to follow our lead, accept your call to action, or whatever the point of your talk is. 1 other words, your presentation should put the audience in a position where you can influence them.

Warmth makes you appear friendly and approachable. On its own,
won't help you be successful. Just being amiable and warm to other peopl
is a nice characteristic to have; however, it's not sufficient. When you marr
it with power and presence, though, you find a balance. You're n(
overbearing, but neither are you a doormat. You become an approachabl
leader, using your influence to help others, not harm them.

Everyone can develop more charisma. You might not be a second Bi
Clinton, but you can increase your presence by being mindful when you ta
to people. Being more confident also brings you more ability to influenc
other people. And even if you're not naturally an enthusiastically cheerf
type of person, you can use body language to appear a bit warme
Developing charisma is about overcoming the obstacles in your way c
improving these three characteristics. I've boiled it down into three steps.

1. **Get comfortable with discomfort.**

   It's normal, and everyone feels it at some time or another. You'r
   no different, so don't let it get in your way. Breathing exercise:
   meditation, surfing the urges all help you stay with the discomfo
   until you can get through it.

   If you have been warm and not powerful, then increasing you
   ability to influence people may feel uncomfortable at first. That
   okay. It doesn't mean you should stop working on it.

2. **Turn your negative thoughts into neutral ones.**

   A thought is just a product of some random brain signals, and it

74

not necessarily true. If you have an inner voice that's always critical, give it a name. It's not you thinking these negative thoughts or being overly critical, it's Negative Nat or Negative Nellie.

When your negative voice appears, you'll know it's Negative Nat talking! Maybe Nat's saying something like, "I can't do this." Turning that into a neutral thought might sound something like the following. "I can't do this now, but I'm going to learn how to do it." "I can't do this now because I don't have the time to tackle it, and that's ok." "I can't do this, and I don't have to if I don't want to."

3. **Find the positive. After you've acknowledged the negative thought, what are the positives to the situation? Can you imagine a way in which things will turn out for the better?**

When Negative Nellie chimes in with, "I can't do this," the positive might be, "I can't do this right this second, but I'm learning how to do it, and in a few months I'll be able to do it." Or, "I can't do this, but I can do something else that makes my life better instead."

None of these suggestions say to ignore the negative thoughts, because at actually doesn't help. Your brain still knows they're there. cknowledging negative thoughts, and changing them to neutral and later, ositive ones, allows you to move through the discomfort.

Breaking down the barriers, or hurdling the obstacles, if you prefer, is ne way to help you develop the charisma you're seeking. There are some ody language moves that can help as well.

Some of them I've discussed in previous paragraphs or chapters. For

75

example, maintain good posture without making yourself smaller. That's power move. Recall that people want to be influenced by someone who ha confidence. Standing tall with an open body without defensive postures is great way to project self-assurance.

Be like Bond, James Bond. Does he aim to please other people? Do yo ever get the feeling he's looking to others for approval? Of course not. He' the movie definition of self-assurance! His posture is regal and confiden not fidgety or needing reassurance. He's a great role model for those wh want to be charismatic without veering into arrogance when they're tryin to increase power. As always, though, aim for balance. Don't overdo it an act aloof or above it all! Remember that power needs to be tempered wit warmth and presence.

A great move to increase your charisma is to mirror the person you'r talking to as long as they're in a positive frame of mind! If they're slouchin and looking away, you don't want to mirror their body language. But yo might still want to mimic a gesture, like a hand movement or taking a sip c water. You might not make the exact same gesture, but amplify it or mak it smaller instead. Reflect the normal gestures that feel comfortable for yo If they're doing something unusual or something that doesn't work wit your body, you don't have to mirror it.

Mirroring others helps you with presence. In order to mimic wh they're doing, you actually have to be aware of it. Staring at your shoes c looking around for the exit means that you'll miss the movements they'r making. Mirroring also increases your warmth, as far as the other person i concerned. We mimic those we like. If you're mirroring them, then yo ıust like them. If you like them, they're more likely to find you warm and ʿiendly.

What if they're angry? You don't want to be mimicking clenched fists ɾ confrontational postures! Break their angry stance by having them hold ɔmething. Offer them a drink. They'll need to unclench their fist to take ʿhatever it is you're offering. Then use your own positive body language. ɪnile, stand tall, and use positive hand motions. Once they've regained ɪeir calmness, you can mirror.

Or maybe you choose to walk away. In the next chapter, I'll go into ɛtail about forging connections with the people you actually want to ɪgage with. Opting not to engage, or develop a relationship with someone ʿho's angry, is a perfectly valid choice for you to make. Rather than trying ɪ shift someone else's mood, you might walk away. See if there's someone ɪse you want to practice increasing your charisma with.

Chapter Summary

- Confidence is the key to public speaking. Fake it 'til you make it! You may need to pump yourself up before the presentation but do so in private.

- Enter the room and walk to the stage like you know where you're going and what you'll do when you get there.

- As you're preparing your speech, consider the body language that should accompany the words. Where can you use gestures or move around? Where can you show emotion? Watch a good speaker on your topic for inspiration.

77

- During the presentation, maintain your body language so that th audience feels engaged and connected with you. Stand tall, approac the listeners, and make eye contact.

- Charisma is a skill you can learn, and it is based on three factor; warmth, power, and presence. Body language can help you improv each of these.

- Learning to be more charismatic means that you'll need to overcom common obstacles like discomfort and negative thoughts.

- To increase your power, use your confident postures: standing ta and walking purposefully.

- To increase warmth and presence, mirror the other person' movements.

We've talked a lot about connecting and engaging with other peopl especially in this chapter. In the next, we'll take these skills and apply the to developing deeper relationships with others.

CHAPTER SIX

Forging Meaningful Connections

onnecting with other people is an important survival skill for human ings. Even introverts need a community! Theirs might be smaller than at of extroverts, but either way, communication with others is key for a appy and meaningful life. Everyone needs some people with whom they ave a deep and reliable connection.

Finding someone to have this kind of meaningful relationship with isn't ways easy. Though this relationship can be romantic, it doesn't cessarily have to be. It may also be a strong friendship where you rely on ach other when things are difficult.

Nonverbal communication is very important for finding people and tting to know them. Being able to read the message someone else is nding lets you know if they're interested in forging a connection with you. nd the more likable your body language is, the more probable it is that u'll be able to connect with someone else.

When done right, body language adds clarity to communication. Tonal ifts, facial expressions, and gestures help to improve the message and ake it more understandable to others. When you first meet people, being le to read their nonverbal signals means you're more likely to get what they're saying. It can also help you decide if you want to spend more time with this person! On the flip side, knowing what body language makes you more (or less) likable can help you attract the right people.

Common cues that other people are sending you

Some body language indicators are very clear in what they express. They're unambiguous, whether the other's emotion or mood is positive or negative. However, others are ambiguous and may take more practice for you to decode them. Here are a few of the tells sorted by clarity and mood:

1. **Clearly positive**

   A (genuine) smile signals that the person is interested in you and what you have to say. If the smile is tight or doesn't reach the eyes, that's a different message!

   People tend to move closer physically to those they like and/or feel comfortable around. Therefore, someone who's interested in what you have to say will probably be near you or move closer to you.

   A gentle (nonviolent) touch, like a pat on the shoulder, also lets you know the person you're talking to is comfortable with you. Depending on your relationship, the touch might be a hug or a pat on the shoulder or arm or back. Ever hugged someone you didn't enjoy being with? Me neither!

   Touch also has some cultural connotations. Americans tend to prefer more personal space, and they're also less likely to use much touch in their conversations. Other cultures need less personal space. They use touching more often with the people they're comfortable with.

Strong, confident stride? Here's a confident person. As long as they're not swaggering, it's not a show of arrogance. Confident people normally look like they know where they're going, whether they do or not!

Moments of joy are expressed by looking upward. This isn't necessarily a signal that you've caused someone joy! However, you might take it as a sign to approach the person. It's much easier to get to know someone who's in a positive frame of mind.

A person who's making eye contact with you is interested in you and wants to know more. When you're talking, and they're looking right at you, take that as a sign you may have a connection waiting!

2. Unambiguously negative

By contrast, not looking you in the eye indicates the other person is not interested, especially when they're looking down or looking around, either for someone more interesting or the exit so they can escape. They might be looking at their phones or even closing their eyes. They won't be smiling a real smile either, though they may have plastered on a fake one.

They may be fidgeting too. Restless hands and feet usually are a sign of boredom. You'll see them drumming their hands on the table or their own legs. They might also be drumming or tapping their feet. If you see someone pacing, change tactics. They're trying to tell you something!

Instead of adjusting what you're doing, you may want to go

elsewhere and find someone who's not so obviously bored by you presence!

If you catch someone rubbing their eyes, they may be tired. On the other hand, they may be sending a message of impatience particularly if they take off their glasses and rub the bridge of their nose.

Rather than being bored with you, another individual may be uncomfortable or defensive instead. Arms crossed in front of them They're trying to shield themselves from you. It's a defensive move that shows you they're not feeling very comfy with you around.

Another clear indicator of nervousness is throat-clearing Sometimes people have colds or allergies that cause post-nasal drip But if their voice is clear and they're showing other signs of nervousness or boredom, it's not a cold that's causing their throat clearing.

When you see someone giving off an angry message, reconsider whether you really want to approach them. It'll be much harder for you to work your body language magic on someone who just isn't having it. Their anger may actually have nothing to do with you. could be the person they were just talking to or a situation they just left. Regardless, it doesn't really matter in the moment whether you're the source of their anger or not. It's much easier to approach someone who's presenting positive signs, as discussed above.

Look out for a person standing with their hands on their hips. They are probably angry, and most likely have lost all patience.

Are their hands bunched into fists? You want to give them a lot of personal space because that's often a sign of incoming violence. If you don't need to interact with them, don't.

You're probably familiar with the idea that little kids stomp around when they're angry, frustrated, or didn't get something they wanted. As it turns out, this behavior is true for some adults as well! If you see one stomping around, they're probably angry or trying to intimidate you. You definitely don't want to try to connect with someone who's stomping at you to scare you away like they would a bear or a feral dog!

3. Ambiguous

a. Hands behind your back

When you see this posture, know you'll need to read some more body language to make sure you're getting the right message.

In the military, standing with hands behind the back is a sign of respect. If you're speaking to someone who is or was in the service, this might be what their body is telling you. Individuals who demonstrate their respect are interested in potentially forming a relationship.

As I mentioned in a previous chapter, showing one's hands is a sign of being open. It shows that you're not carrying a weapon, which is what it meant hundreds of years ago. It's a signal of vulnerability that shows you're confident enough to walk toward another person without being armed.

Therefore, if someone's hands are behind their back, what are they hiding? It may be an indicator that the person isn't trustworthy. They may be interested in forming a relationship with you, but you migh not want to reciprocate.

On the other hand, not showing your hands can also be seen as sign of power. In this case, hands behind the back signals a perso who's trying to dominate the people they're speaking to. In othe words, no thanks, they're not particularly interested in what yo have to tell them.

b. Pushing or jutting the chest out

This particular gesture tends to be gender-specific, although bot genders will push out their chests for both reasons.

Men are usually pushing out to intimidate others. Just like many c our animal kingdom cousins, they're trying to look bigger as a wa of showing their power. They want to look strong. This is often a attempt to intimidate other males. But it can also be a nonverba communication to attract women.

Women typically push out their chests to attract men, rather than fc intimidation. But they sometimes use it as a power play, too.

c. Staring

The messages behind this specific body tell are pretty similar t those for jutting the chest out. It may not be gender-specific, but th reasons for dominance or attraction are the same.

The other person may be staring at you because they find you attractive. They want you to stare back in return or respond in some other positive way.

Or, they may be staring at you because they're having a power contest. The first one to break the stare loses. The dominant member of the pair doesn't break first.

Whether the stare signals dominance or attraction, it's usually pretty obvious to the receiver what the message is. If not, other body language cues will help you determine what the person staring at you is trying to say.

d. Cocking the head to one side

Often, a head tilt indicates confusion. Ever seen those pictures of dogs where a human is talking to them, and they're tilting their heads from side to side, trying to understand? The same goes for humans, though we noticeably look less lovable or goofy when we do it.

However, cocking your head slightly may signal interest. Someone who's tilting their head as you talk and not looking confused or lost may simply be telling you that they're interested in what you have to say.

Hopefully, most of the readers of this book won't need to worry about this last message that a head tilt might be sending! In locations where there's usually plenty of violence, like jail or a pro wrestling ring, cocking the head is a challenge.

People connect with people they like, so use your body to increase your likeability

Not sure that likeability is key for relationships? Well, let me ask you question. Do you have a deep urge to forge a link with someone you actively dislike? Probably not! Just as you don't usually hug people you're no friends with, you don't connect to people you're not friends with either. An other people behave in the same way.

At a minimum, most individuals need to feel comfortable with another person to genuinely relate to them. If you're looking to make more connections or deepen the ones you already have, you'll need to ensure the people feel comfortable around you, which means that you're likable an open. If you seem defensive or nervous or closed off in some way, other can't feel comfortable around you. They won't feel they can get to know you.

Of course, meeting new people to develop those new relationships is no easy and may be even more challenging for introverts. Making other comfortable in your first meeting gives you a better chance to create connection over time. As an introvert, you'll be satisfied with just a few close relationships. You prefer not to interact with people you don't know more than absolutely necessary. Therefore, if you can start relationship with like-minded individuals right away, you'll be able to build you network more quickly. As a bonus, this means you don't have to go meet new people as often!

If you're an extrovert, being likable on the first meeting just means you have the opportunity to cultivate more relationships. You won't have t

86

end as much time developing the relationship because you start off strong, begin with.

Whether you're an introvert, extrovert, or ambivert, you can use onverbal communication to make people more comfortable with you from e very first meeting.

But before you can be likable, you need to be presentable. That doesn't ean you have to go to your networking event in your best ballgown or xpensive tuxedo, unless that's how your industry dresses, of course!

What it does mean, however, is that you, your clothes, and your ccessories need to be clean. This includes teeth, nails, and hair. Again, I'm ot saying that your teeth must be blindingly white or that you need a salon ppointment every time you go to an event! However, you don't want eople waving their hands in front of their faces because your breath is so ad, or your nails look like you were digging up bodies right before you got ere. A good haircut is helpful, but at the very least, your hair should be ombed.

In some cases, it's alright to dress more casually. Flip-flops, shorts, or pped jeans (as long as everything's clean!) may be acceptable. If you're ot sure, wear nicer clothing like trousers with a button-down shirt. If ppropriate, dresses are sometimes good for events, and they're easy to wear s well. Make sure that your shoes are not scuffed, dusty, or dirty before ou go.

In addition, avoid having a strong smell, whether you think it's a good ent or a bad one. If your body odor is bad, take care of that before you go.

87

But don't douse yourself in perfume or after-shave either! Many people ar sensitive to fragrances, and they won't find you particularly likable if you cologne is giving them a migraine.

Now that you're presentable, follow up with positive body language fc success. Warmth is essential for people to like and trust you, as I discusse in the last chapter about charisma. Make good use of body language tha helps you demonstrate warmth and trust.

While this book is specifically about nonverbal communication, hav you ever heard the advice to talk less about yourself and ask more about th other person? People like to talk about themselves. They like to feel tha others are interested in what they have to say. When they're talking mor about themselves, paradoxically, they'll feel friendlier toward you! They'r doing something pleasurable, so their brains are rewarding them wit pleasure chemicals. And you're there, now associated with these pleasar feelings.

As always, though, you do need a balance. If they've heard this advic too, they'll want to know about you. When you're asking questions, try n to fire them off like you're trying to interrogate them! That doesn't fee warm and friendly to them.

Being associated with the brain's pleasure chemicals is where you war to be when you're talking to someone you think you'd like to connect witl Whether or not the other person is aware that it's happening, or the exac mechanism that you know about from reading this book. Fortunately, yo can create this effect with nonverbal communication too. Here are ten way to make the individual you're talking to feel good about themselves an ou.

1. Genuine smile

Funny how this one comes up time after time when discussing body language! If you only have time to invest in a few ways to talk without words, then work on your smile. No blinding white, perfectly straight-toothed grin is necessary. Just a warm smile that says, "I am glad to be here with you right now."

A genuine smile doesn't flash briefly. You hold it while approaching someone, so they know it's sincerely aimed at them. When you're having a conversation, smiling continues to convey warmth.

2. Positive touch

Some people are not as open to physical touch, but this is a powerful method of communication. It signals that you're comfortable with the other person and feeling warm toward them, which makes them feel warm and comfortable toward you in return.

In other words, when it comes to a lot of body language messages, do unto others as you would have them do unto you!

Would you give your enemy a pat on the back? Or briefly touch the arm of someone you didn't really care for as you spoke to them? Of course not. This communication is reserved for people you actually like.

One of the hormones that also acts as a neurotransmitter is oxytocin. It encourages bonding between humans and is released when you touch or are touched by another person. It's also thought t encourage trust between people when circulating throughout th brain. In the body as a hormone, oxytocin tends to help individual relax and reduce stress and anxiety.

Therefore, you can see why touching other people can be s powerful! It promotes the release of a chemical that helps others d pretty much exactly what you want! Be calm and stress-free, so the find you comfortable to be around. As always, don't overdo i especially when you don't know the other person. Too muc touching might be interpreted as creepy, not bonding.

Make sure your handshake game is on point as well. Shaking hand is another opportunity for you to project warmth and openness, a well as confidence. But don't offer a feeble handshake. A wea handshake makes you look weak, which is not what you're goin for when meeting new people.

You don't want to crush the bones in their hands either. That' aggressive and dominating. Just as you don't want your audience t feel you're trying to dominate them when you're giving presentation, you don't want people you're meeting for the first tim to feel that way either. A firm, respectful shake is all you need.

3. Good but not rigid posture

Many of these body language signals are easy to remember whe you think about your goal: make other people comfortable aroun you and see that you're open and warm.

When you see other people looking uncomfortable, does that make you feel better or worse? It's hard to feel comfortable when someone else is obviously uncomfortable!

Well, have you ever seen someone standing rigidly in position? Maybe in a military parade, or even in a movie? Does it look comfortable? No way. Did you feel like you wanted to approach them and get to know them better? Nope! They don't come across as warm and friendly or open and interested.

By contrast, when you see someone slouching, do they come across as likable? Or confident in themselves? Would you rather get to know someone who's not self-assured? Or is it easier to get to know someone who's confident (but not cocky)?

Right. Good posture that isn't rigid reads as friendly and approachable. You're not worried that you're going to have to keep shoring up a slouching person's self-esteem if you get to know them better. Nor do you think the person is too closed off by rigidity to want to get to know you.

Someone with good posture comes across as self-assured. Humans tend to prefer getting to know confident individuals because they seem like they know what they're doing, and we like that quality in our friends and romantic relationships. We certainly like competency at work. If you have a colleague or boss who's incompetent, it can be even worse than if they weren't there at all. People are drawn to leaders who are confident, not those who seem wishy-washy or unsure of themselves.

91

If you've got good posture and you read as confident, you'll attrac more people. You might not want to build connections with or ge to know all of them, but at least you'll have better opportunities t find those with whom you can have a meaningful relationship.

4. Face the other person completely: face, torso, hands, legs, feet

As I mentioned above, it's a quirk of human nature that we lik people who visibly demonstrate an interest in us by asking question about ourselves and not talking too much about themselves!

Therefore, when you're not showing your interest in someone, the will likewise not be interested in you. Make sure you're not givin off signs of boredom. Avoid giving the impression that you'd rathe be anywhere else but here talking to this person.

In the last chapter, we discussed how important presence is fc charisma. Being fully present is the only way to truly engage wit another individual. They need that feeling that, at that moment, yo would rather be talking to them than anything else. Your bod language needs to show that.

Have you ever spoken to someone who seemed like they reall wanted to be there talking to you? Where were they facing? You, c course. Would you think they'd lost interest by turning their fac away from yours? Of course. But they also turned their bodie toward you.

Had you looked down (which you might not have at the time), yo would have seen that their feet were pointed right at you. It' impolite to point fingers, but they were probably turning their hands toward you as well.

They weren't shielded from you, crossing their arms over their torso or holding an object between the two of you. Their bodies were open, showing they were comfortable with you. If they'd been feeling defensive, you'd have seen it. Removing the barriers shows that you're open and unafraid to trust them.

Crossing legs is a defensive posture, too, so the person happy to talk to you is standing straight with their weight evenly planted between their feet. Good posture! They're confident and open talking to you.

You can use these tools when you're trying to make others feel comfortable and interesting. Don't cross your arms or legs. (If you have to go to the bathroom, excuse yourself and then return!)

Avoid any other barriers between their body and yours. This isn't restricted to just arms and notepads, but could even be something like a desk or a table. If you want the other person to feel at ease, you might need to move out from behind furniture in order to give them the open body that represents trust.

Aim your feet at the other person and not, say, the exit or anyone else in the room. If it's a crowded room, you might need to lean in to hear them better.

5. Maintain good eye contact

Like smiling, making eye contact is a key signal that you're open and interested. It gets you pretty far in many social situations.

93

Looking around, down, or side to side is a signal that you're no interested in them. It makes you seem like you're looking fo someone better to talk to, or that you're not self-assured, or that yo don't want to be there talking to them.

If the person you're talking to says something or asks a question tha you need to think about, it's fine to break the eye contact so you ca think. Many of us think better when we're looking up or at a poin in the distance. Once you're ready with your answer, make ey contact again when you deliver it. If you're still staring off into spac when you start talking, you'll be giving the impression that you'r bored with them.

Staring creepily at the person you're speaking with is also problem. Feel free to blink when you need to!

A lot of the body language tips, and situations where you need then are designed for when you're standing, be it in front of an audienc or socializing at a networking mixer. But there are times when you' be seated, for one reason or another. If you need to take notes, mak sure you're not writing so copiously that you lose eye contact.

Also, writing too much will make the other person wonder what is, exactly, that you're writing! Taking too many notes appea sinister, not friendly. Jotting down notes is one thing, writing th Great American Novel when you're supposed to be talking t someone is another.

Avoid looking at your watch, your smartphone, the clock, or the re of the room while you're having a conversation. You want them to feel that you're interested in them, which automatically makes you more interesting to them! But if you're looking away, you're signaling that you don't care about them.

People often ask what to do when they're expecting a call. Taking calls in the middle of an event is pretty rude. But if your conversation runs over, or you just met someone you'd really like to get to know, let them know in advance. This shouldn't be something that you do a lot. If you're constantly taking calls at a time when you're usually socializing, you need to work out a better schedule.

6. Use gestures—appropriately

Can you imagine being best friends with a robot? I can't, either. Gestures are a very human and non-robotic way to communicate with other people. Most people have gestures that come naturally to them as they speak, so they shouldn't hold back.

As with eye contact, you need a balance. Flailing or using exaggerated gestures makes you look weird or out of control. When you're out in public or social events, your movements should appear deliberate.

Researchers found that the most popular TED talks are the ones where the speaker used a lot of hand gestures. In fact, the most-watched speakers averaged nearly double the gestures per talk than the least-watched ones!

You may not be giving TED talks, but people clearly prefer those

who use more gestures. And not just during presentations, but als
in more casual conversations. We had hands before speech, s
talking with our hands is a pretty universal human characteristic
Robots don't talk with their hands.

One thing to watch out for is whether your gestures are appropriat
from the audience's point of view. For example, if you're discussin
a rise in prices, your natural instinct is to swoop your hand up fror
left to right. But that's backward for your audience. Swooping u
from right to left looks correct to the people facing you, even thoug
it's backward for you.

Huge or exaggerated movements make it seem like you're stretchin
the truth. Keep your moves authentically small. If you're a perso
who naturally uses bigger gestures, you don't need to make ther
tiny if that's not how you typically use your hands to "talk."

Gestures clarify and add impact to what you're saying. They ca
make you seem interesting when you use them to punctuate you
story or conversation. Don't be afraid to use them, within reason.

7. Avoid restlessness

Just as windmilling around like a crazy person doesn't engende
trust and comfort in the people watching you, neither does fidgetin
At least you won't seem to be a lunatic, but you will come off a
being nervous.

Nervousness is off-putting, or at least not very likable, for a lot c
people. Many of us prefer to be friends with, or close to, people wh

demonstrate some confidence in themselves. It makes the other person wonder if it's their fault that you're so nervous. No one wants to feel like they're the ones doing something wrong!

Are you comfortable when the person you're talking to is fidgeting? They might be playing with their hair, rapidly clicking a pen, shifting their weight from foot to foot, tugging at their clothes, or otherwise demonstrating that they're not comfortable, in which case you become uncomfortable as well.

Stillness has a certain authority to it. It makes you look more confident. People who are bobbing their heads or wriggling around look nervous or ill at ease, which doesn't promote trust in the other person. So, plant those feet. If you need something to do with your hands, try steepling them, which is also a pose of confidence and prevents you from fidgeting with them.

8. Mimic the other person

Ever heard the phrase, "Imitation is the sincerest form of flattery"? What better way to indicate your interest and trust in someone else than by copying their movements when you're with them?

You don't have to act like a human mirror. This isn't an acting lesson! You can (and should) reflect some of their positive or neutral gestures. Are they smiling? You probably should, too. Have they taken a sip of their drink? Go ahead and try yours.

You can make your gestures a bit smaller than theirs as you don't want to overdo it. Also, you don't want to mimic them if they're giving you angry postures: hands on hips, clenched fists, etc. You want them to feel good around you, which means you need to feel good around them. Imitating someone else's negative body language is going to make you feel more negative.

9. Make sure you're on the same level

If you're sitting on a chair that's higher than where they're sitting for example, you'll appear to be domineering. Or if you're standing and they're sitting. At the same time, you don't want to be at their feet either. That makes you seem too needy.

If you're a short person, sitting down is often your best move. People won't tower over you quite as much when you're both seated. Standing on a nearby stool will also help, but it looks like you're trying too hard! Sitting to talk also works well on the other end of the spectrum, if you're very tall. You don't want the people you're conversing with to feel like you're looming over them. When you're both sitting, the height difference is minimized.

In a situation where everyone's seated around a table? Try to sit on the side and not at the head or foot. This helps people let their guard down around you. You won't seem aggressive or dominating but like one of the others. If you're in a room full of mutual strangers, taking an end seat reads as if you want to take control of the group, which is normally not appreciated.

10. Think of everyone in the room as a friend

If you haven't introduced yourself to someone before, they're

98

simply a friend you haven't met yet! Are you warm and approachable with your friends and people you know well? Go and be likewise with new people.

This is an especially good tip for introverts, who often feel dread at the prospect of so many new people. Opening yourself up to others as potential new buddies encourages them to reciprocate. Now you have become their friend they just haven't met yet! And it takes the edge off a roomful of people you don't already know.

Extroverts may be doing this already. After all, what better way to relax and project confidence, than by assuming everyone in the room is or will be your friend?

However, not everyone is going to like you. And that's OK.

You can master all these body language messages and use them every me you're at a social event. There will still likely be people who don't ciprocate. They won't smile back. They won't point their feet toward you, ven as you've pivoted your whole body to them. If they shake your hand : all, it'll be brief and probably limp. Their eyes will dart around the room, eeking someone else to talk to.

Most of the time, this really has nothing to do with you personally. Iaybe you look like the person who broke their heart ten years ago. Your cial features are just like those of the math teacher who made them iserable in eleventh grade. You sound just like their father, with whom ey have a difficult relationship. Your name is Ben, and a boy named Ben illied them all throughout middle school.

99

And so forth. You get the picture. What should you do about it? Mayb over time, you could help them feel better about their mathematic abilities! Get Ben to apologize!

No. Let them go. Your job is not to save or fix other people. (They migl be proud to be estranged from their abusive father.)

Instead, form relationships with others who are interested in doing th same with you. Care about connecting with people who are willing t connect with you. The other person's issue is not a challenge for you t conquer. You don't get a medal for forcing someone to like you. Conside their inability to see you as the wonderful person you are as their loss. Mov on.

You might be comfortable already with some or all of these helpf techniques. If not, practice with friends, family, and coworkers. It mig help for family and friends to understand what it is you're trying to do. Bu you may not want to share it with your coworkers.

For example, maybe you decide to try mirroring your boss. They take drink; you take a drink. They're fond of steepling their fingers; you sta steepling your fingers. Not only might this help you develop your bod language skills, but your boss might start to like you if they don't already

Reach out and touch someone!

How to tell if someone else is lying to you

No one wants to be taken in by someone who's not telling the truth. It embarrassing and might cause others to question your judgment. Bod language is very helpful when you're sizing someone up to see if you mig ant to develop a relationship with them. They might be saying all the right ords, but you'll see some red flags waving.

Being deceitful is usually signaled by a change from the other person's aseline. This is their usual body language when they are truthful. When ou're familiar with someone, you're familiar with their baseline as well.

But you can still judge when someone else is being deceitful, even when ou don't know them well or even at all. If you've been practicing the iggestions in this book, you can observe how they behave when you ask iem a good baseline question. You'll be maintaining eye contact and atching for their nonverbal communications.

A good question to determine baseline is something like, "Where are ou from?" or "How did you hear about this event?" These types of iestions usually don't result in a lie. Their answers and how their body ssponds should give you a pretty good idea of their language when not ing.

There are four major shifts in the body language of liars that give them way. The movements are often bodily expressions of what they're doing hen they're fibbing, such as hiding, distracting, and trying to prevent the uth from slipping out.

Remember, these movements all need to be taken into context. Someone ho's fidgeting may just be nervous, not lying. The other signals they're nding you will let you know whether they're untruthful or simply anxious eople.

101

1. Body movements

Lying can actually be hard for our brains to do. When the brain busy coming up with a story, there may not be enough bandwidth t gesture and talk at the same time. Therefore, one of the signals tha someone is not truthful is that the hand gestures come *after* the speech, not during it. They've had to manufacture the movemer after they manufactured the story for you.

People fibbing tend to use both hands when they do the gestur Truthful ones often use just one hand. Here's where you really nee to understand the baseline, because some people (and cultures) tal with both hands, not just one. An individual using both hands ma be of a different culture, not a liar.

The liar may keep their palms out of sight, in their pockets, or behin their backs. Are they hiding something from you? Yes! These ar classic "hiding" movements.

They also may fidget, squirm, and play with their hair while they'r talking. These actions are reflecting their need to distract you fror the truth.

2. Facial expressions

People not telling the truth may stare or look away at a momer when you would otherwise expect them to be making eye contac Lips may disappear or be pursed during a lie.

Pursing their lips often signal that the speaker doesn't want to sa whatever it is they're saying. Or, at least, their brains don't. Fibbin requires more energy because the tale has to be constructed. Our brains would prefer to use less energy, so telling the truth is easier.

Disappearing lips often signal a lie by omission. The speaker is trying to hold back something like facts or emotions.

Turning pale is often a clue to a lie, as blood drains from the face. Excessive sweating or signals of dryness can indicate deceit, too, depending on the person. Liars may find that their nervous system provokes T-zone sweating.

For others, the lie might cause dryness in the lips and eyes instead. This results in too much lip-licking or blinking, which are pretty obvious signals to look out for. If someone goes from rarely licking their lips at baseline to suddenly licking every three seconds, that's a strong signal for you.

3. Tone of voice

Stress tightens the vocal cords. You might hear a liar's voice being higher than normal.

It could also be louder, as people tend to pump up the volume when they're feeling defensive. Liars are often feeling defensive about the tale they're telling, but someone who isn't lying might have a reason to be defensive. They're not feeling comfortable around you because you remind them of that math teacher, and so their volume goes up.

4. What they say

If words like "honestly," "frankly," or "let me tell you the truth"

come out constantly ... methinks they doth protest too much! Lia
are also likely to add more placeholders like "um," "ah," and "er.
Listen for slips where they accidentally let the truth out!

Trust and your body language

In contrast, you can show people that you're trustworthy and hone
with your nonverbal communication skills. There is a lot of overlap betwee
body language that you use to increase your likeability and body languag
you use to convey your honesty. Trustworthy people are more likable tha
those who aren't, and vice versa.

1. **Open body**

   Just like making someone interested in you consists mainly of yo
   showing interest in them, being trustworthy has a lot to do wit
   showing your trust in the other person. You're not defensive, so you
   arms and legs aren't crossed. Nor are you shielding yourself fro
   the other person with a table or item held between you.

   They can see your hands. Liars hide their hands, so you don't. A
   noted in an earlier chapter, palms up is a supplicating gesture. Palm
   down is a more confident way to hold your hands. You might choos
   steepling here too. You do want your hands to be open and relaxe
   not clenched or tense.

   You're looking at them, not away from them like you're bored o
   hiding something. Your expression is neutral or friendly. As alway
   a smile goes a long way too.

2. Deliberate movement, including mirroring

Eye contact! Steady, that is not a stare or frequently flicking away. No bobblehead figurines either. Trustworthy people are usually assumed to be strong and confident, so showing weakness or a lack of self-assurance makes you look less trustworthy.

Likewise, make sure you're not flailing or making sudden moves. Your gestures should be slow or moderately paced if you're a person who operates at a faster speed than others. Movements should be intentional. People also tend to read smooth movements as more trustworthy as opposed to herky-jerky ones.

Mirror their actions, though not so precisely as to be robotic. You want them to feel that you're aligned with them, not that you're simply a mirror in human shape.

3. Demonstrate concern for the other person

Tilt your head, or even your body, forward to show that you're listening and would like to hear more. Touching someone gently often expresses concern, particularly if they're emotional. In addition, as I discussed above, touch releases the body chemical that promotes bonding and trust in human beings.

Eyebrows are a great tool too. You can use them to show surprise by raising them. Furrowing them indicates concern.

4. Show respect

If you want respect, you have to show it to others! Being attentive to them is key, so you're listening to what they have to say, mayb

slowly nodding along. (Nodding too fast suggests annoyance mor

than respect.)

Don't crowd the person you're talking to, especially when you don

know them. Bear in mind the cultural issues around personal space

Having said that, moving closer is a sign of interest in the othe

person.

Put your phone down! It's hard to be more disrespectful than to pu

your phone out and disengage from the conversation right in the

person's face.

Be an influencer in person

How do you become the most memorable person in the room? Hin

body language has a lot to do with it! Research shows that there are fou

nonverbal ways you can increase your influence. With verbal speech, the

are three methods: ask open-ended questions, so they talk about themselve

tell stories, not fibs; and ask for a favor, known as the Ben Franklin effect

But let's "talk" body language.

1. Give your audience a dopamine hit

In Chapter One, I talked about dopamine, which is

neurotransmitter released when the brain recognizes pleasur

Whatever it is, the brain wants you to do that again! If the oth

person's brain releases dopamine as you're talking to each othe

you're now associated with pleasure. Their brain wants you to b

around because you have a pleasurable effect on them.

It's similar to the effects of oxytocin, as described in this chapter. When they get the oxytocin release and feel calm and relaxed around you, they'll associate you with that calm and relaxed feeling. Most of us don't need any more stress in our lives! They'll find you likable because you appear to relieve their stress.

But how do you get that wonderful neurotransmitter release in someone's brain? Connect with them emotionally. You might want to have some questions prepared like, "What are you currently working on that you're passionate about?" "What was the best part of your day?" This stimulates the emotional connection between the two of you. Once they're talking, you can respond appropriately without even using your words. Smile, frown, or nod, and mirror their gestures.

2. Display confident body language

Just as you wouldn't slouch when you're walking into a room or giving a presentation, don't slouch in front of someone you'd like to influence. No one wants to be led by an individual who appears nervous or unsure of themselves.

Much of what you learned in Chapter Five about public presentations also applies to speaking to people you want to influence. Projecting confidence is important. You don't want to bobble your head, tug at your clothes, look away from them or around the room, cross your arms or legs, clench your fists, hide your hands or put them on your hips, arms akimbo.

Stand up straight and firm, without being rigid or shifting you weight from foot to foot. Smile. Offer a firm handshake. Keep you hands in an open position where the other person can see them. Fac the person you want to influence with your torso and feet as well a your face and arms. Maintain eye contact. Use your hands to hel clarify and emphasize the points you're making verbally.

Gestures and signals that demonstrate confidence are great t practice any time you're in a social situation. Even if you'r speaking with someone you don't necessarily want to influence, tr out all these confidence postures. Act as you would if you wer trying to influence them. See what happens!

3. Show vulnerability

When you show other people that you trust them, by bein vulnerable, they will find you more likable and trustworthy. Neve underestimate the value of being real! People can relate to you (an find you more likable) when you show you're just another huma being with flaws. No one relates to a robot or someone who eithe seems perfect or seems to think they're perfect!

Displaying emotions is a way to show vulnerability. Think abou James Bond again for a moment. Does he appear vulnerable? Nc often. Does he show emotion? Not often. Anger, maybe. But h doesn't have much of an emotional range.

Which is fine if you're a superspy trying to destroy the evil villain before they destroy the planet. But if, as I suspect, that's not yo (apologies to James Bond if he's reading this!), then showing your emotions allows people to connect with you.

This also may be something you need to practice, especially if you're not someone who already tends to wear their hearts on their sleeves. If you start feeling sad, let that show on your face. Feel the emotion in your body, and let your body reflect it. Yes, you might slump a bit temporarily or look down at your feet.

You might be thinking this sounds completely contradictory to what was said before, about being confident and standing up straight and smiling! That's certainly how you want to greet people and present yourself in front of a crowd. That should be the first impression that you make.

But when you're listening to someone's story, or even relating your own, it's OK to allow the emotions to surface and express themselves non-verbally. If you need to take a moment, take a moment.

4. Be more charismatic

Increasing your influence means that your effect on others is positive and important. You've probably assimilated the news by now: people like those who make them feel good about themselves. Fortunately, this is another skill that can be learned. Some people do seem to come into the world with an innate sense of how to make other people feel important. But the rest of us, well, we'll need to put in the work.

As Maya Angelou said, people may not remember the words yo say or the actions you performed, but they will remember how yo made them feel. Charismatic people make others feel good throug both their verbal and nonverbal communication styles.

If that doesn't make sense to you, think about the people wh influenced you—a parent, a religious leader, a coach, a teache someone you've never met but read or heard about. How did the make you feel? Inferior or less-than? Incompetent or incapable?

It's certainly possible that you were influenced negatively. An adu told you you'd never amount to anything, so you worked hard an achieved just to spite them! It happens. But more often, people ar influenced by the people who made them feel good, the people wh told them that they could do it, that they were capable and equal t anyone else on the planet.

To be charismatic (also discussed in the previous chapter), you nee to be present with the person you're conversing with. Not lookin away or paying attention to anything or anyone else. You're focuse on what they're saying, leaning in a bit to hear them better an indicate interest. Your torso and feet are pointed toward you audience, signaling that you want to be there conversing with thei and not somewhere else.

Charisma also includes power, in the sense of influencing other Here's where self-assurance is your best ally. You project th impression that you know what you're doing, and you know wher you're going. You avoid signs of nervousness and anxiety-lik

110

fidgeting, shifting from one foot to another, or tugging at your clothes or hair. You've got some authority in keeping your head still as you speak, not bobbing up and down or side to side.

The third characteristic of charisma is warmth, which also increases your likeability. If you're displaying raw power, that might come off as aggressive: not pleasant and warm. Nodding and smiling as appropriate when you're listening to someone else brings out the warmth in your persona. Warm body language signs also include an open body, hands with the palms showing, and plenty of hand and arm gestures.

Once you've practiced your influencing skills, make sure you use your ower for good, not for evil. Influencing others in a positive direction will ot only make them feel better, but it'll make you feel better as well. We e social creatures after all, and assisting others in our group, however that ay be defined for each of us, makes us feel better. We get our own opamine and other neurotransmitter "hits" when we're helping other eople.

Chapter Summary

Connecting with others on a deep level is an important tool for human irvival. We evolved to have relationships with others whether we're more omfortable with just a few close connections as introverts or plenty of them extroverts. Body language is key to developing these meaningful lationships with others. It clarifies our message and demonstrates our own ustworthiness as well as our likeability and interest in others. In turn,

111

they'll want to forge better relationships with us.

- Some body language, both positive and negative, is clear. Other cue are more ambiguous. Context is often important in decipherin unclear gestures such as putting hands behind the back, staring, an jutting out the chest. It's also useful in situations where cultur: differences may muddy the message.

- People want to connect with others whom they like and trus Increasing your own likeability helps you to build relationships wit others, even when meeting for the first time. There are ten ways t increase your likeability and demonstrate trustworthiness wit nonverbal communication alone. These include a warm, genuin smile; open and confident body language; and mentally acceptin everyone as a friend you just haven't met yet.

- Not everyone will like you, and that's alright. It may have nothing t do with you as a person. It's not a challenge to overcome or a opportunity to "fix" someone else. You're better off using your tim to find people who are interested in you and visibly want to get t know you better.

- You don't have to like everyone else, either, particularly if you thin they might be deceitful. Fortunately, you can spot a fibber throug their body language. You'll see unconscious differences compared t their usual baseline nonverbal behaviors. Liars tend to change i terms of body movements, facial expressions, tone of voice, an words they say. However, it's also possible that someone displaying these behaviors because they're uncomfortable and nervous for some other reason, not because they're actually lying.

- By increasing your connection with others, you can increase your influence. There are seven methods to be more memorable, and four of them are nonverbal. These include showing vulnerability through emotion, connecting emotionally, and encouraging positive neurotransmitter release through your body language.

The next chapter brings you actionable steps to communicate onverbally in your everyday life. Whether it's to improve the nderstanding that others have of your message or to build better elationships with others, if you practice consistently, your skills will nprove.

4. Pose for the camera if someone is confrontational

Supermodels rarely face the camera head-on. They're usually at an angle. Normally, face on and open to the other person is a way to be warm and trustworthy. But sometimes this can seem threatening or confrontational. Maintain eye contact, but shift slightly, so you're at an angle to the other person.

If you can manage it, standing side by side is a collaborative pose. This may be helpful if the other person's threat level doesn't decrease with your angle posture.

5. Gesture, but no higher than your shoulders

Instead of talking *to* the hand, talk *with* your hands! More gestures make you more energetic and add to your likeability. Also, the more you fall into the rhythm of moving your hands, the more easily your conversation happens.

Movements above your shoulders look odd, so avoid that. You can still do plenty of gesturing without flinging your hands up to the sky.

6. Make *them* move

A good way to engage others, especially if they're defensive or slouching, is to get them to move. For example, if someone is sitting with their arms crossed (a typical defensive posture), ask them if they want a drink, or if they can hold your pen while you're pulling out your business cards.

In front of a group? Maybe you can ask questions to get them to

117

raise their hands. Pass items around the room. Maybe even get them up from their seats to do something. You might find they're initially resistant to standing for what seems a silly exercise. You'll also notice when they sit back down how much more relaxed and open they are!

7. Look away to think before you speak

Typically, when someone asks a question where you need to think about the answer, you'll look away while you're thinking, be upwards, to the side, or studying your feet.

Make sure you return to your open, standing tall posture before you answer. Hold eye contact as you're answering, even if you had to break it while you were thinking. Not maintaining eye contact while you speak reads as being shifty or hiding something.

Using body language to improve your own life and character

Nonverbal communication isn't just between you and other people. There are feedback loops between your actions and your brain. For example we discussed smiling above. Changing your body language to incorporate smile also changes your body, soothing stress. There are other moods and characteristics that you can improve just by adjusting your communication with your own self!

1. Increase sincerity

Using the power of touch more often, and more consciously, at least at first, shows the person being touched that you're sincere in what you say. In fact, you can convey emotions quite well using just the

118

touch of a hand on another's arm!

2. Supercharge your creativity

A lot of readers are going to LOVE this one! Need to be more creative and innovative? Lie down! I'm not sure your boss will approve you moving a bed into your office, though.

This is thought to be caused by the neurotransmitter norepinephrine, further discussed in Chapter One. More of it is released when you're standing, and it tends to inhibit creativity.

3. Build your (willpower) muscle

By flexing your physical muscles! Doing so not only helps you better handle negative information but also helps you resist unhealthy foods and habits.

4. Nevertheless, you persisted

The idea that crossing your arms is a defensive mood is pretty well-known. What you may not know, however, is that doing so actually helps people stay with difficult problems longer. So, if you're feeling stuck on a project, cross your arms.

This is one you might prefer to do in private, so it doesn't give the wrong impression. Crossing your arms can also decrease nervousness.

5. It's a bird, it's a plane, it's...you

Power poses increase confidence. Like crossing your arms, these are best done out of sight of others. But stand like Superman, legs spread, hands on hips. Feel that confidence grow! It's good for an time you need a little boost.

6. Relieve your stress

Activate positive feedback loop, go! Target: smile. It helps decreas the amount of cortisol in your blood, which makes you feel les stressed. Your audience will start feeling less stressed, too, as yo smile, and they smile back. Instead of a negative downward spira of stress, spiral upward with a smile.

7. Get comfortable

Is your friend someone that you're always a little uncomfortabl with? Probably not. You're comfortable with your friends and vic versa. The more comfortable someone is with you, even if they'v never met you before, the more likely they are to like you.

Best of all, there's a simple little trick to it. Tilt your head forward bit when you're introduced to someone. It lets them know tha you're happy to meet them, which makes them more inclined to lik you. That's reflected in their body language to you, making you fee more comfortable.

It's that upward spiral you're looking for!

8. Better understand someone else's emotions

Sometimes, when you're trying to connect with someone, you migl have difficulty empathizing. You'll find improvement just b mimicking them.

It's a slightly different feedback loop compared to the others. Mirroring another's body language is mirroring their emotions, which in turn generates those emotions for you.

People are also more likely to befriend someone whose facial expressions are reflecting theirs. So, you'll actually help boost some positive emotions for them, even if the ones you were mirroring weren't so positive.

9. Work it, supermodel

Ease the tension by standing at an angle to the person who is possibly challenged or threatened by what you have to say. Or if they're confrontational already.

Shift your feet so you stand like a supermodel, not facing the camera (or the other person) head-on. It's a less adversarial pose than standing face to face, especially if the faces are way too close together!

10. Retain what you learn

As it turns out, kids learn better when they use their hands. This works for adults too! It's an alternative way to cement new information into memory.

11. Feel like a cheerleader

Not feeling happy and upbeat? Pom-poms won't help, but chewing gum will! (For the sake of your teeth, choose the sugarless stuff.) It can make you more alert, plus help you focus your attention. And put you in a better mood.

Naturally, you don't have to do all these things separately, although yo can as well! Stuck on a tough problem? Lie down, cross your arms, an chew some gum. Feeling nervous before a networking mixer? Stand lik Superman out of sight, then smile and tilt your head forward when meetin new people.

Improving your body language literacy

Nonverbal communication clues are complex. Someone may b demonstrating several cues at one time, all of which have differen meanings! There are general rules that can be used in most cases, thoug the context is always a concern. Most people who study nonverba communication do so only briefly, and so they don't take the time to lear these messages and retain them.

However, the ability to read other people's nonverbal language is a ski that can be learned. It's definitely a use-it-or-lose-it type of knowledge, s daily practice is your friend here. Reading it and using it effectively boi down to a few key points.

1. **Awareness**

    The first thing is to understand some basic nonverbal messages an how they're sent. In the beginning, you may not even be aware c the signals that you're sending, much less what they mean. How d you express emotions?

    Learning about cues can help with your own body languag development as well as helping you better read what others a

122

"telling" you.

2. Desire to learn

With no particular reason to care about nonverbal cues, it's easy to get away without learning very much. However, someone who really wants to make deep connections with others, be a superstar presenter and speaker, or ensure that they're sending clear and unmistakable messages will reap the benefits of studying this "language."

3. Receive feedback

Sometimes, especially in the moment, it's hard to see what our bodies are actually doing, especially when we're earlier on in the awareness process. Are you really being energetic? Or are you closing off without realizing it?

Feedback is important for you to understand the message that you're actually sending, not just the one you think you're sending. Also, it will help to ensure that you're reading someone else correctly.

If you don't have a mentor or colleague that's willing to help, use your friends and family as a sounding board.

4. Practice, practice, practice

It's not just how you get to Carnegie Hall! As noted above, nonverbal communication is a skill that needs to be maintained over time. It's not something where you can have an AHA! moment and suddenly stop slouching forever! (Your mom will agree with me.)

Instead, try these techniques as much as you can. As you've rea
this book, or even this chapter, you've learned quite a few eas
actions to take. You know by now that standing tall (not slouching
increases confidence. Go ahead and sit up straight right now,
you're seated.

You know that a (genuine) smile has a positive feedback loop effec
Smile. When the delivery guy comes to the door, tilt your hea
forward. When your uncle becomes belligerent over th
Thanksgiving holiday, stand at an angle to him if you feel the nee
to tell him why he's wrong.

Nonverbal communication is like many other skills: the more ofte
you work them, the better you get at them. Were you perfectl
balanced the first time you got on a bike? What happened the firs
time you drove a car? The first time you got in the water, were yo
an instant champion? Even Olympic swimmers need to practic
practice, and practice some more.

You may never be the most memorable person in the room. Yo
may never get to the point where you can tell what someone's goin
to say before they even open their mouth. But you can be mo
memorable. You can be better at understanding what someone els
is saying. You can make your own messages clearer.

Improvement is better than nothing!

EQ: as important as IQ

Most people are familiar with IQ, or intelligence quotient, as a measu

’ your smarts. But are you familiar with EQ, or emotional quotient? here’s no standard EQ test out there. Emotionally intelligent people nderstand their own emotions and can empathize with others too. EQ is an nportant skill to develop whenever you want to improve your relationships ith others or even with yourself since, as with smiling, there’s a feedback op between your expressions and body language and how you feel.

There are four components of your EQ that relate directly to body nguage.

1. Self-awareness

To be able to read and understand other people, you have to first do so for yourself. What are your triggers? What are your avoidance or defense mechanisms? What do you tend to do when you’re tired/irritated/frustrated? It’s the ability to view yourself almost as if you were a different person. Not-you can see what makes you tick.

When you’re self-aware, you can see if your nonverbal communication is sending the right message. Do you want to appear confident? See if you’re standing tall, with your head held high.

2. Self-management

This is your ability to regulate your actions. You may be tired, bored, and frustrated, but you don’t always want to show that. Even if you feel like hitting out, either physically or verbally, you restrain yourself.

Obviously, if you can’t take control of your actions, you won’t be able to communicate nonverbally in the way you want. Maybe if you're frustrated, you smile, knowing that it has a positive feedbac loop.

3. Other-awareness

Hopefully, after reading this book and practicing, you hav improved your ability to read other people. You can be sensitive t the needs and feelings of others and react accordingly.

Much of being able to read other people is found in body languag Emotions are most commonly expressed nonverbally, and you nee to be able to pick up on these cues. You'll understand their messag as well as where they're coming from.

4. Relationship management

Are you able to interact well with other people? The better you a at relationship management, the better your relationships tend to b Whether you're an introvert and run with a small crew, or a extrovert with plenty of phone numbers when you need to tal having a social network is key to human happiness.

In terms of body language, you'll need to change and adjust you posture and gestures as the situation demands.

Five emotions tend to come up in relationships, especially at worl There are common expressions of these five that you can learn to recogniz

5. Confidence

Do you have a confident colleague? Someone who always or almo always gives off an air of self-assurance? Think back to how you'v

126

seen them behave. They likely walk with a strong stride and offer a firm handshake. They're relaxed, with an open body and free gestures. They maintain eye contact in a way that suggests they want to hear what you have to say.

6. Nervousness

In contrast, do you know anyone who blinks or looks away a lot? That doesn't read as confidence, does it? They're more likely to offer you a flaccid handshake than a firm one.

Their stride is uncertain, and when they're standing (or sitting still), you probably see their arms crossed over their chest pretty frequently.

7. Defensive

These people also tend to cross their arms over their chests! Nor do they look you in the eye, though they are more likely to look down at the ground. If they move their hands at all, the gestures are muted and small. Their hands are clenched, and so are their faces! Both are tense and tight. They probably turn away from you too.

8. Bored

This person has no interest in listening to you or what you have to say, so they're hardly making any eye contact, if at all. They may have a glazed or blank stare in their eyes, and their pencils are busy doodling, assuming they're not face down in their phone, that is.

They won't sit up straight but instead slouch when seated.

9. Thinking (prior to speaking)

Breaking eye contact isn't always a bad thing. It could just indicat that the person is thinking. If so, they're often looking far away int the distance where the answer is, or looking up.

There are a lot of head and hand gestures that people use whe thinking. In addition to looking away, their heads tilt at an angle They might be stroking their chin, resting it on their hand, or restin a cheek on their hand.

Once they've completed their thinking, their eyes will return to you

Chapter Summary

The ability to read body language, and to match your verbal messag with your nonverbal one, takes practice.

- Nonverbal communication is very much a use-it-or-lose-it type c skill.

- There are seven ways to practice communicating in your dail routine, including shifting your position if the situation become confrontational and looking away to think before you speak.

- You can use body language in eleven different ways to change c improve your own character and mood. Power pose to increase you confidence, cross your arms to get through a difficult problem, an chew some gum to increase your alertness.

- There are four ways to improve your ability to read body language on a daily basis, and these methods include receiving feedback and having a sincere desire to learn.

- Because body language often expresses emotions, the higher your emotional intelligence (EQ), the better you'll be at interpreting what others are "saying."

- There are emotions and moods that often appear, such as boredom and defensiveness; they all have signals you can learn to recognize, such as lack of eye contact and what people are doing with their arms.

CONCLUSION

ody language is an important part of the communication between two uman beings. Why do people find it so easy to misunderstand emails and xt messages? Because the body language doesn't come through! Even lking on the phone is better, because the tone of voice is an important clue) the message of the person talking. In the absence of nonverbal ommunication, conversations are liable to misinterpretation.

Being able to read another individual's body language depends first on eing aware of the messages that you're sending yourself. After reading this ook, you might have realized that you often slouch, giving off the npression that you're not confident. Or maybe you cross your arms over our chest, which makes you seem defensive.

Fortunately, as you've discovered, nonverbal communication also llows you to communicate messages to yourself as well! If you want to el more confident, you decide to stand in a power pose for a minute or two private, legs spread wide and hands on your hips. You opt to smile when ou're feeling grouchy, knowing that smiling tells your brain that you're appy.

Using your own body language supports you when you're trying to olve difficult problems. When you're stuck, you lie on your back and cross our arms over your chest, since these movements increase your etermination and creativity. Just what you need to figure out the answer!

Many people find speaking or presenting in public a terrifying prospec But in this book, I shared the secret with you: fake self-assurance. You no know how to use confident body language not only to boost your ow confidence but also to be more appealing to your audience. You may nee some power poses in secret backstage first, but you choose to stride firml up to the podium or dais. You stand tall with your body open, making ey contact with audience members as you talk. Your weight is planted firml on both feet, so you're not rocking or bobbling.

Any movements you make are done so consciously. You use your hand to emphasize and communicate. Once you're comfortable enough with you material, you also move out from behind the podium and approach th audience. You know to stand still to make your point, and only then mov again. And you smile because you know people respond to warmth an friendliness.

Many of these same techniques are also handy when you're meetin people for the first time. Faking confidence is still perfectly fine becaus you will end up with more self-assurance over time. Faking it makes yo feel more confident, so you're able to charm more people, which makes yo feel more confident. Think upward spiral.

People want to get to know those individuals that make them fee comfortable and welcome. You provide a firm but not crushing handshak and tilt your head forward, indicating interest when you meet someone You're open to them, not using your arms or anything else to shield you body from the person you're talking to. Maintaining eye contact, you no appreciatively, and get them talking about themselves, which is everyone'

132

vorite subject and makes you instantly more likable!

Now that you're aware of your own nonverbal communications and ave been practicing your own movements, you can use those same skills read other people better as well. Understand what they're actually saying d even feel what they're feeling by mirroring their movements.

You can tell someone is closed off from you when they're not facing ou with their whole body and their arms (and maybe their legs too!) are ossed. Or perhaps they're holding their purse or briefcase in front of them a shield. If you do want to forge a connection with them, you'll need to t them to open up first. Hand them a drink so that they have to uncross emselves.

You can also opt to move on. You might have the friendliest, warmest, ost charismatic body language out there, and still have someone dislike ou. In the interest of saving time or finding someone who truly is interested what you have to say, you can start with someone else entirely.

A person who wants to hear more from you will be smiling a genuine nile and facing you with their arms, feet, and body. They'll be looking you ght in the eye and look relaxed as opposed to tense.

If you do find someone who's tense, angry, or frustrated, you'll see their sts clenched. You don't want to get too close because that will be read as nfrontational or threatening. So, you choose to stand at an angle like ou're a supermodel. You're still facing them, but not completely head-on, hich diminishes the threat level. Assuming you don't avoid this person ntirely, which is also a good option!

133

The number one takeaway

If nothing else, remember that nonverbal communication is a skill tha can be learned. It's not something you're born with necessarily. Wit practice and feedback on a regular basis, you can improve your own bod language and your ability to read that of others.

You can practice with friends and family. If you have friendl colleagues at work, bring them in as well. This way, you can receiv feedback as to whether or not you're sending or interpreting messages a intended.

You can also practice reading people when you're out and about. Yo might not get the feedback, but you'll still reinforce what clues you' looking for. You should be far enough away that you can't hear what peop are saying to one another. Study their body language. Defensive? Bored? it a couple who just had a huge fight or a couple that's enjoying their tim together?

Practice makes perfect, and it can be fun too! Nonverbal communicatic is a skill that can deepen your relationships with others, make you a bett speaker and communicator, and make you a better friend and colleague t others.

REFERENCES

- An, S. (2019, March 27). "7 Body Language Tricks to Become Likeable in the First Meeting." Retrieved from: https://www.shoutmeloud.com/body-language-tricks-become-likeable.html

- Bradberry, T. (n.d.) "15 Body Language Blunders That Make You Look Bad." Retrieved from: https://www.talentsmart.com/articles/15-Body-Language-Secrets-of-Successful-People-2147446605-p-1.html

- "Body Language: Six non-verbal ways to command attention." (2019, February 20). Retrieved from: https://www.creativeboom.com/tips/body-language-six-non-verbal-ways-to-command-attention/

- Bortnicker, C. (2011, March 4). "What Steve Jobs' Body Language Means for Apple Stock." Retrieved from: http://www.minyanville.com/mvpremium/what-steve-jobs-body-language/

- Fletcher, J. (n.d.). "The Important Connection Between Body Language and EQ." Retrieved from: https://www.linkedin.com/pulse/important-connection-between-body-language-eq-joan-fletcher

- Fremont College. (2018, March 8). "How to Read Body Language - Revealing Secrets Behind Nonverbal Cues." Retrieved from: https://fremont.edu/how-to-read-body-language-revealing-the-secrets-behind-common-nonverbal-cues/

- Haden, J. (2018, May 17). "8 Powerful Ways to Improve Your Body Language." Retrieved from: https://www.inc.com/jeff-haden/8-powerful-ways-to-improve-your-body-language.html

- Haden, J. (2018, May 17). "Science Says These 11 Body Language Secrets Will Make You More Successful." Retrieved from: https://www.inc.com/jeff-haden/science-says-these-11-body-language-secrets-will-make-you-more-successful.html

- Haden, J. (2019, February 19). "A Body Language Expert Analyzed Popular TED Talks to Uncover the Top 5 Nonverbal Cues." Retrieved from: https://www.inc.com/jeff-haden/a-body-language-expert-analyzed-popular-ted-talks-to-uncover-top-5-nonverbal-cues.html

- "Harnessing the power of body language to deliver captivating speeches and presentations." (2015, May 27). Retrieved from: https://www.bytestart.co.uk/body-language-speech-presentation.html

- Henry, Z. (2015, May 14). "5 body-language tricks of billionaire entrepreneurs." Retrieved from: https://www.businessinsider.com/body-language-of-successful-people-2015-5?international=true&r=US&IR=T

- Hindy, J. (2018, January 3). "Top 20 Body Language Indicators." Retrieved from: https://www.lifehack.org/articles/communication/top-20-body-language-indicators.html

- "How to engage your audience with the right body language." (2016, May 13). Retrieved from: https://wisembly.com/en/blog/2016/05/13/engage-audience-body-language

- Jalili, C. (2019, January 25). "How to Tell if Someone is Lying to You, According to Body Language Experts." *Time.* Retrieved from: https://time.com/5443204/signs-lying-body-language-experts/

- Kahnemann, D. (2011). *Thinking Fast and Slow.* New York: Farrar Strauss Giroux.

- Kinsey Goman, C. (2012, February 13). "Seven Tips for Effective Body Language on Stage." *Forbes.* Retrieved from: https://www.forbes.com/sites/carolkinseygoman/2012/02/13/seven-tips-for-effective-body-language-on-stage/#41048061536d

- Kinsey Goman, C. (2018, August 26). "5 Ways Body Language Impacts Leadership Results." *Forbes.* Retrieved from: https://www.forbes.com/sites/carolkinseygoman/2018/08/26/5-ways-body-language-impacts-leadership-results/

- Krauss Whitbourne, S. (2012, June 30). "The Ultimate Guide to Body Language." *Psychology Today.* Retrieved from: https://www.psychologytoday.com/intl/blog/fulfillment-any-age/201206/the-ultimate-guide-body-language

- Laliberte, M. (2017, September 29). "8 Ways to Use Body Language to Build Trust." *Reader's Digest.* Retrieved from: https://www.rd.com/advice/relationships/body-language-trust/

- "Leadership 101: How to Command Respect Through Body Language." (2009, June 17). Retrieved from: https://www.comparebusinessproducts.com/fyi/leadership-101-how-command-respect-through-body-language

- Matthews, N. (2015, February 19). "How to Act Like the Most Powerful Girl in the Room." *Elle.* Retrieved from: https://www.elle.com/life-love/tips/g25706/how-to-fake-confidence-body-language

- Mejia, Z. (2018, September 6). "What Sheryl Sandberg's and Jack Dorsey's Capitol Hill testimony can teach anyone about reacting under pressure." Retrieved from: https://www.cnbc.com/2018/09/06/sheryl-sandberg-jack-dorsey-body-language-tips-congressional-hearing.html

- Misner, I. (2013, March 7). "4 Body Language Cues You Need to Know When Networking." *Entrepreneur.* Retrieved from https://www.entrepreneur.com/article/227257

- Misner, I. (2018, July 11). "How to Display the Ideal Body Language When Networking." *Entrepreneur.* Retrieved from: https://www.entrepreneur.com/article/315358

- "9 Powerful Body Language Tips To Instantly Boost Your Confidence." (2019, April 11). Retrieved from: https://liveboldandbloom.com/10/self-confidence/confident-body-language

- Oakey, M. (2017, April 12). "How To Speed Read Body Language With Igor Ledochowski." Retrieved from: http://www.yourcharismacoach.com/blog/how-to-speed-read-people-master-hypnotist-igor-ledochowski-shares-his-secrets/

- "Parts-of-the-body language." (n.d.). Retrieved from: http://changingminds.org/techniques/body/parts_body_language/parts_body_language.htm

- Patton, M. (2014, December 19). "7 Scientifically Proven Steps to Increase Your Influence." *Entrepreneur.* Retrieved from: https://www.entrepreneur.com/article/240960

- Riggio, R. (2011, June 15). "Reading Body Language: It's Not Easy, But You Can Improve." *Psychology Today.* Retrieved from: https://www.psychologytoday.com/intl/blog/cutting-edge-leadership/201106/reading-body-language-it-s-not-easy-you-can-improve

- Roysam, V. (2016, November 8). "3 Things You Didn't Consider While Reading Body Language." Retrieved from: https://yourstory.com/2016/11/3-body-language-misconceptions

- Sheffield, T. (2016, June 10). "9 Body Language Tips That Make People Want To Be Around You More." Retrieved from: https://www.bustle.com/articles/166064-9-body-language-tips-that-make-people-want-to-be-around-you-more

- Study Body Language. (n.d.). Retrieved from: http://www.study-body-language.com/

- "The Charisma Myth: Summary & Review." (n.d.). Retrieved from: https://thepowermoves.com/the-charisma-myth/#Charismatic_Body_Language

- Thomas, J. (2018, July 28). "Unconfident Vs. Confident Body Language." Retrieved from: https://www.betterhelp.com/advice/body-language/unconfident-vs-confident-body-language/

- "Trustworthy Body Language." (n.d.). Retrieved from: http://changingminds.org/techniques/body/trustworthy_body_language.htm

- Wertheim, E. (n.d.). The Importance of Effective Communication. Retrieved from: https://docplayer.net/9673598-The-importance-of-effective-communication-edward-g-wertheim-ph-d-northeastern-university-college-of-business-administration.html

YOUR FREE GIFT IS HERE!

Thank you for purchasing this book. As a token and supplement to your new learnings and personal development journey, you will receive this booklet as a gift, and it's completely free.

This includes - as already announced in this book - a valuable resource of simple approach and actionable ideas to mastermind your own routine towards a more calm and confident way to tackle your everyday.

This booklet will provide you a powerful insight on:

- How to formulate empowering habits that can change your life

- Masterminding your own Power of 3

- Just the 3 things you need to drastically change your life and how you feel about yourself

- How to boost your self-esteem and self-awareness

- Creating a positive feedback loop everyday

You can get the bonus booklet as follows:

To access the secret download page, open a browser window on you computer or smartphone and enter: bonus.gerardshaw.com

You will be automatically directed to the download page.

Please note that this bonus booklet may be available for download fc a limited time only.

Printed by Amazon Italia Logistica S.r.l.
Torrazza Piemonte (TO), Italy

27694366R00087